*To Patti
Happy Tails!
Sandra Bolan*

Dogs and Dads

Photos by Sandra Bolan
Edited by Jackie Lindsay and Brian Balogh

© Copyright 2005 Sandra Bolan

All rights reserved. No part of this publication may be reproduced, stored in a retrieval system, or transmitted, in any form or by any means, electronic, mechanical, photocopying, recording, or otherwise, without the written prior permission of the author.

Printed and bound in Canada by
First Choice books
#2, 460 Tennyson Place
Victoria BC V8Z6S8
www.firstchoicebooks.ca

Dedicated to my boys — Dave, Wally and Alvin.

All we expect from him is to sleep and eat,

but he gives us so much more.

I don't know what I would do without him.

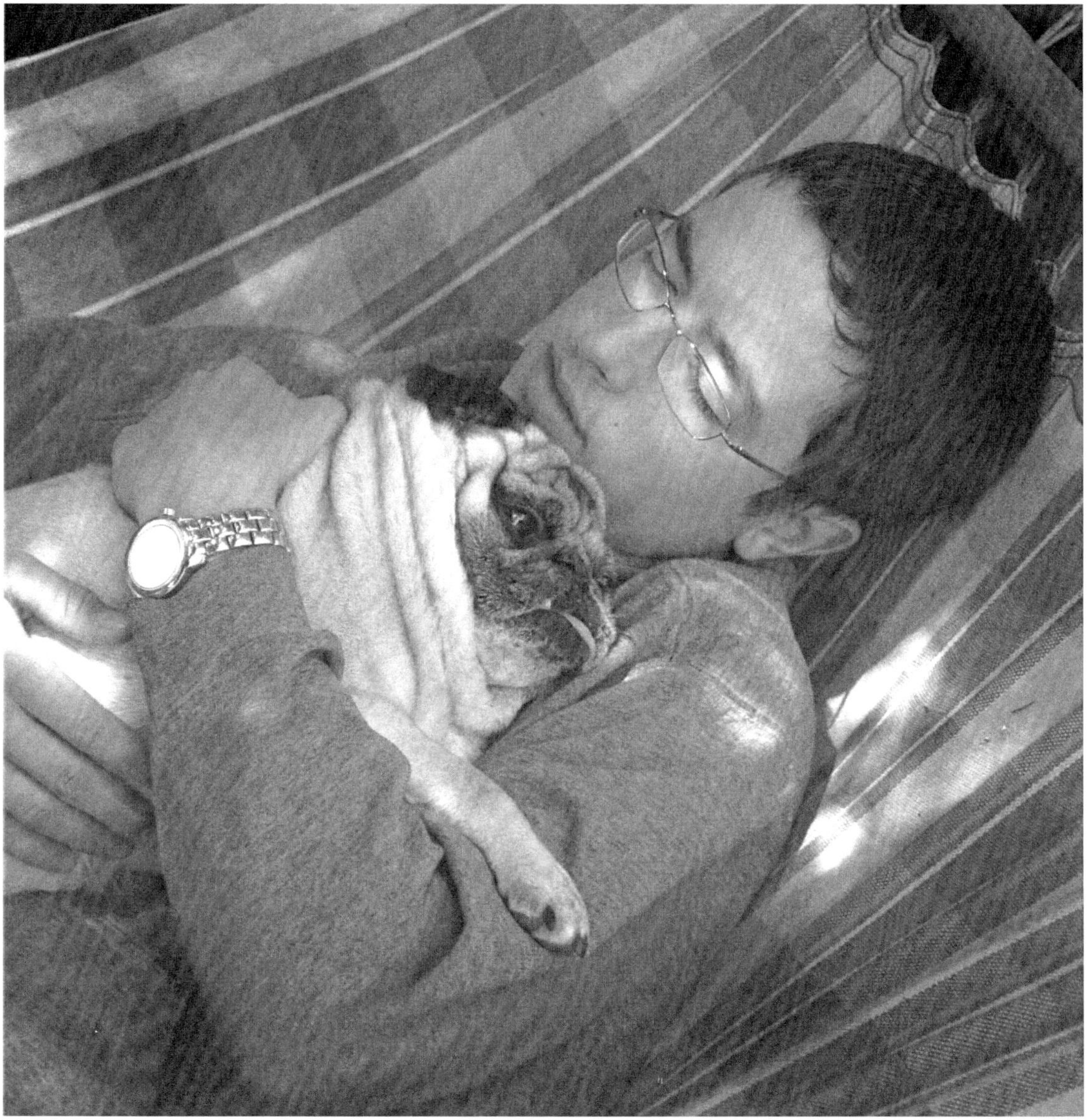

Despite Skye's blindness,
she sees me as her protector and best friend
- as long as I don't re-arrange the furniture.

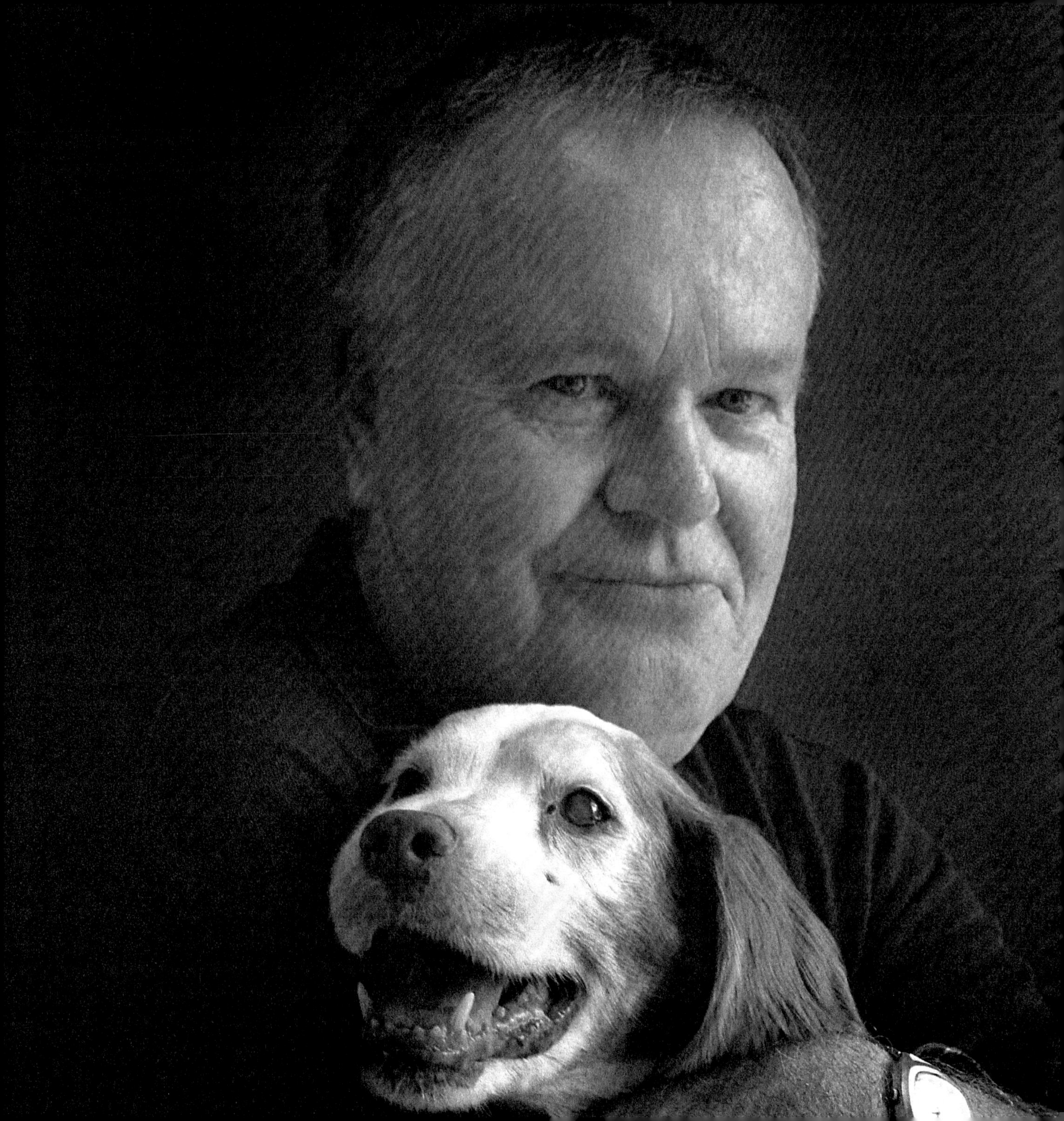

Dogs are the most loving, faithful creatures. They have shown us what patience and love can really do and that it's never too late to trust a worthy human.

I know this little angel
was sent to me by a higher power.

I always thought there was no time
to think about the present.
Since living with Jessie,
she's taught me there's no time
BUT the present.

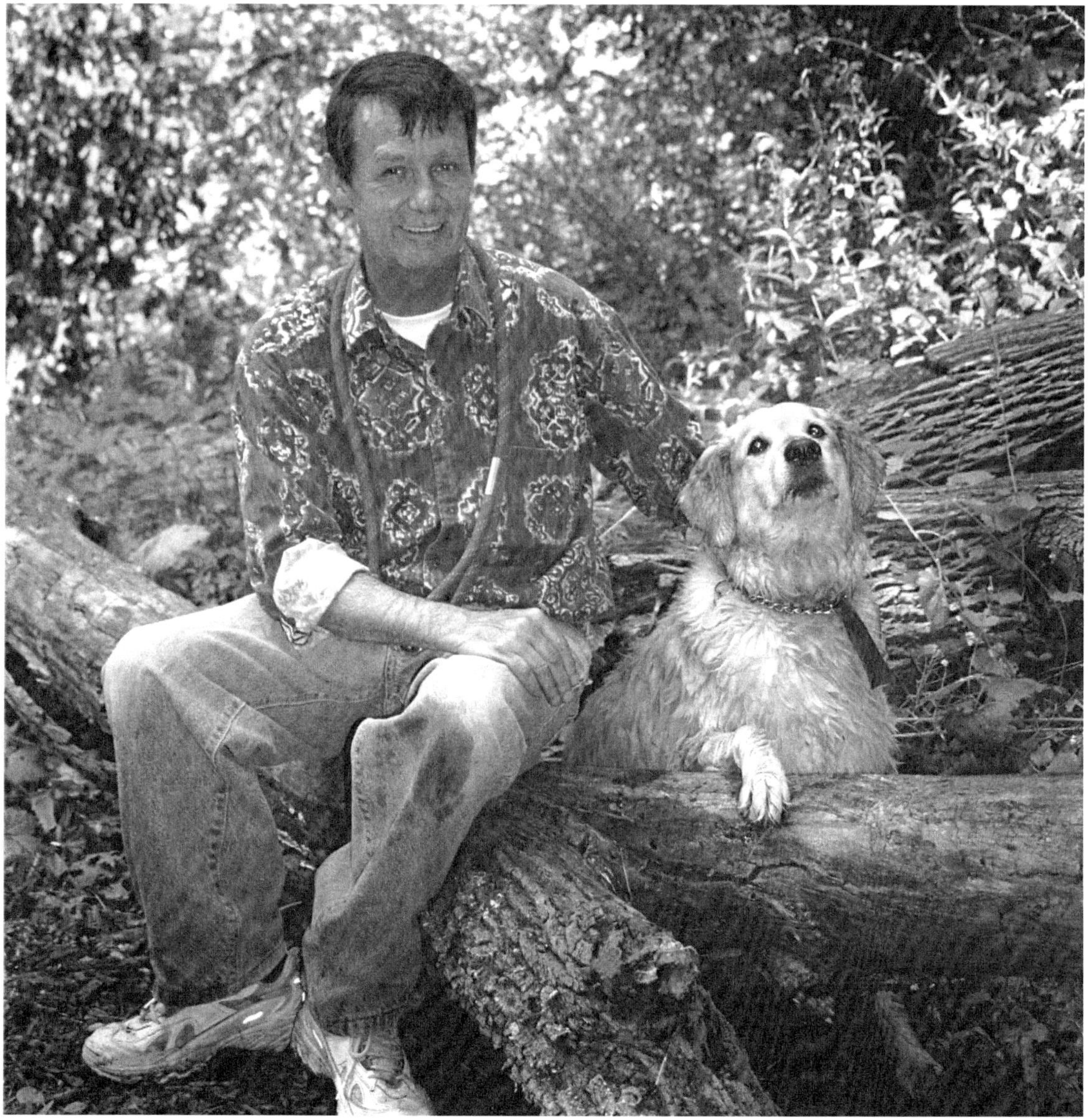

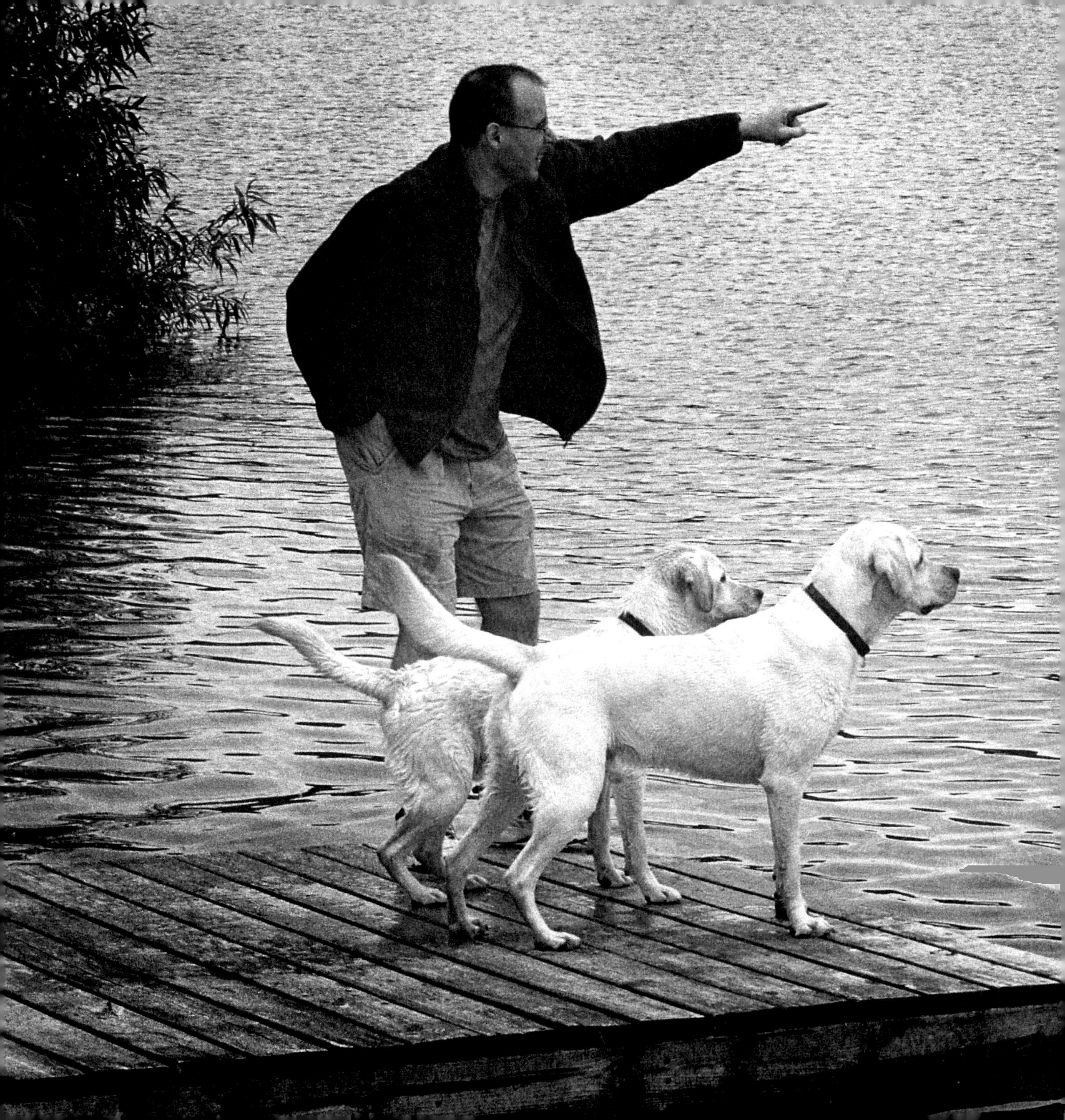

Retrievers bring back what is thrown,
sometimes they just need a little direction.

Give me my dogs,
the off-leash area of a beach,
a nice strong coffee
and I'm blissfully happy.

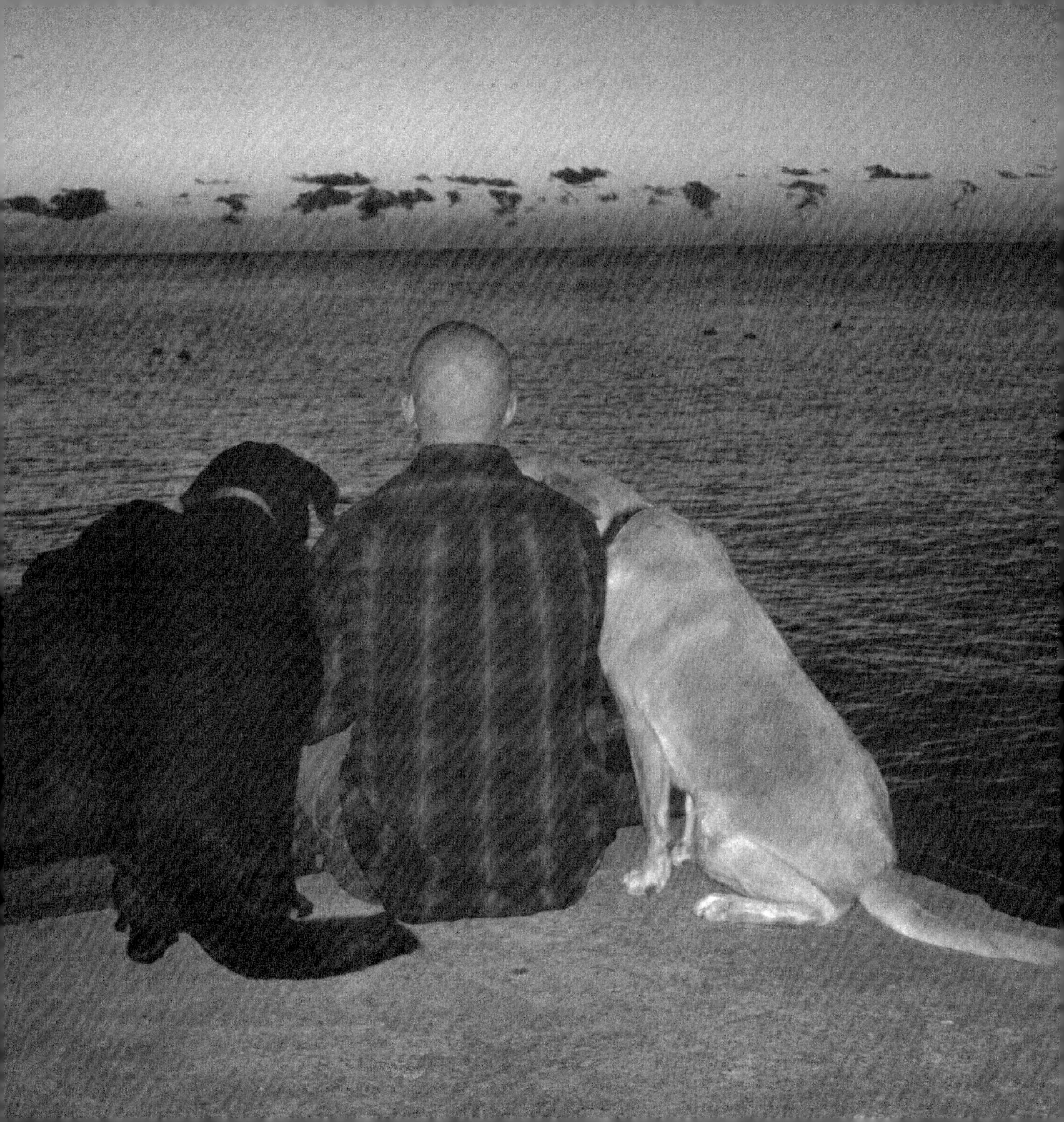

Two sisters,
two distinctly different personalities,
with one human
somewhere in the middle.

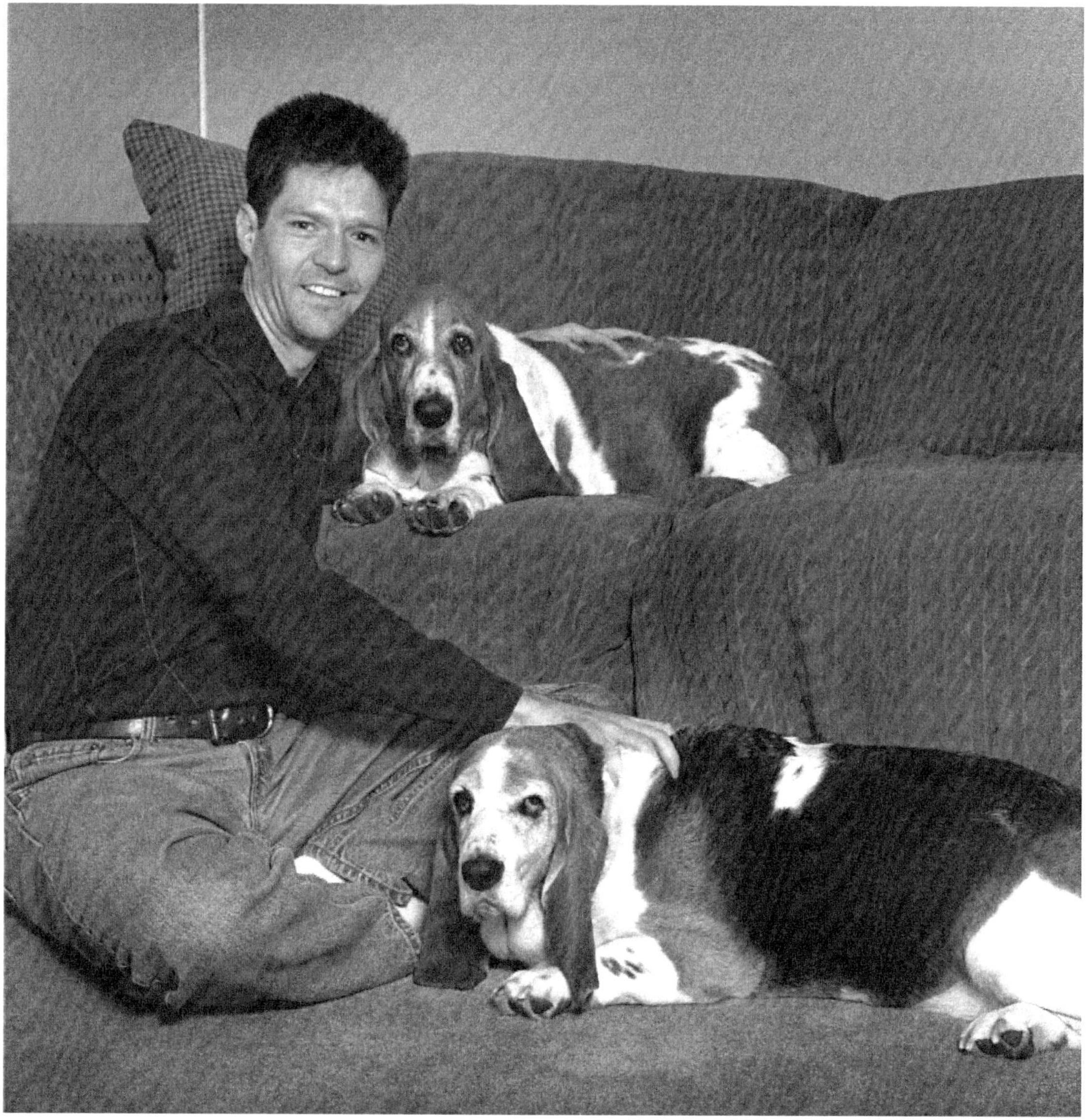

Embrace life.

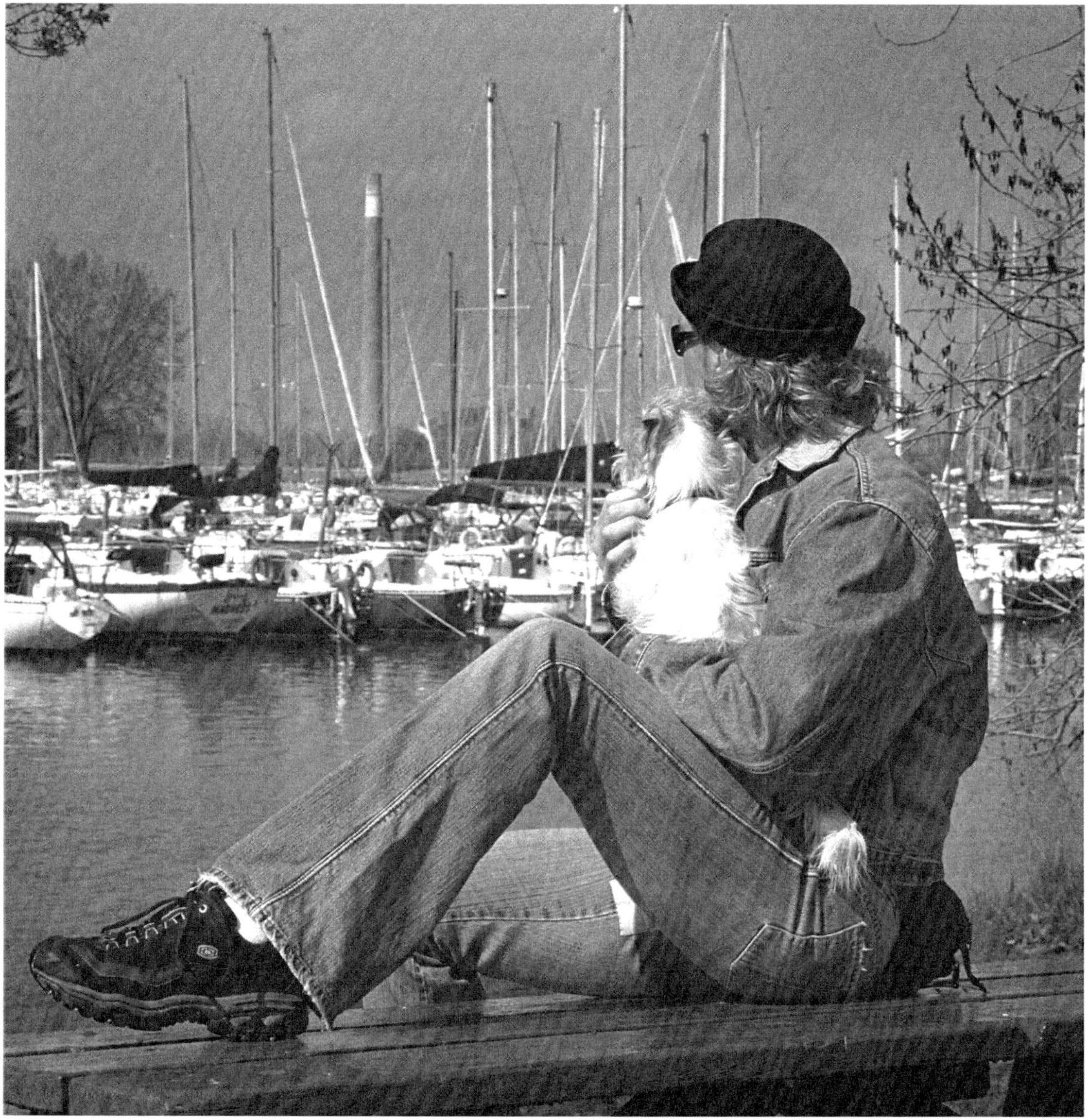

You always stand taller
with a dog on your shoulder.

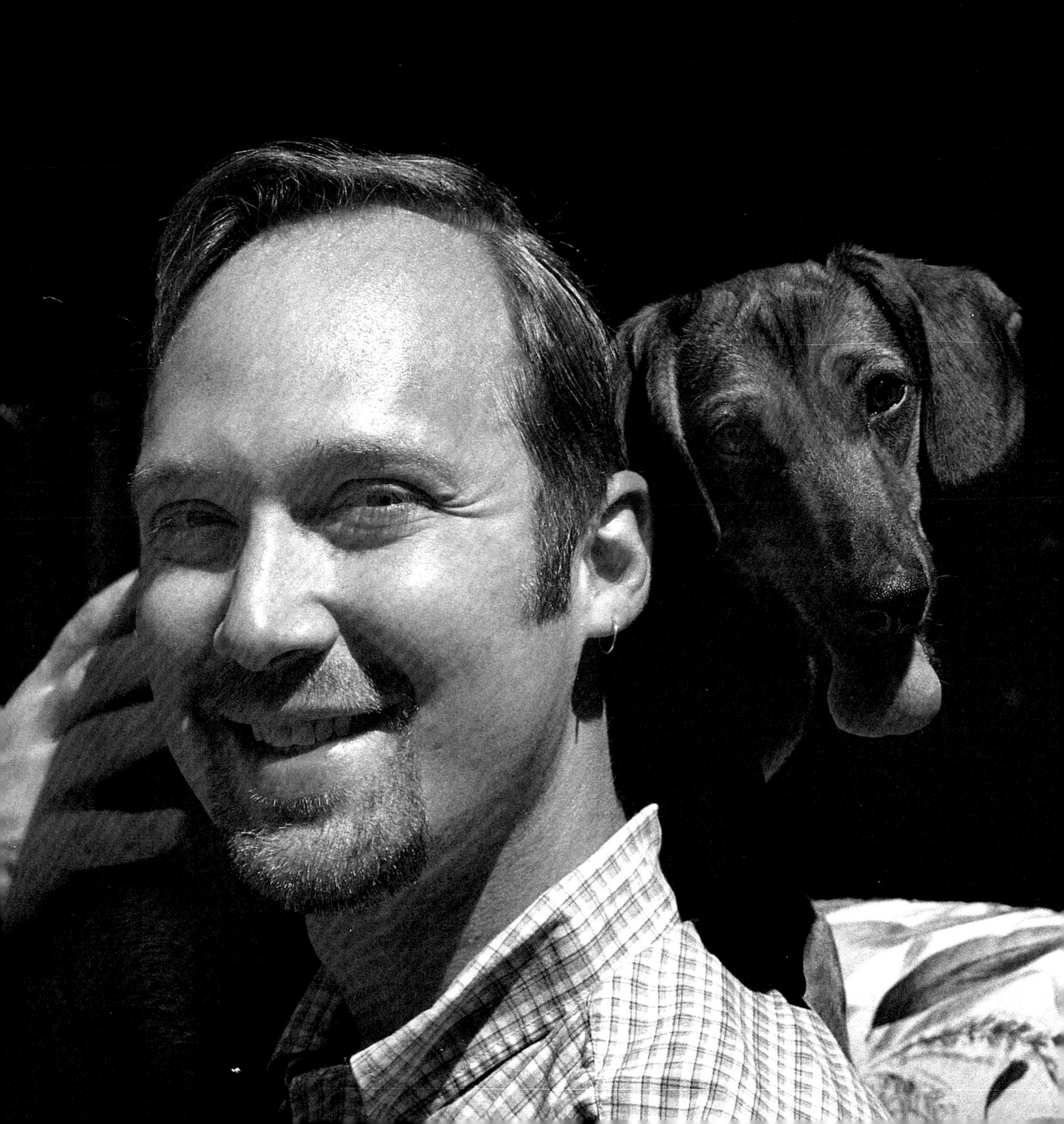

Never under estimate the comforting power of dogs.

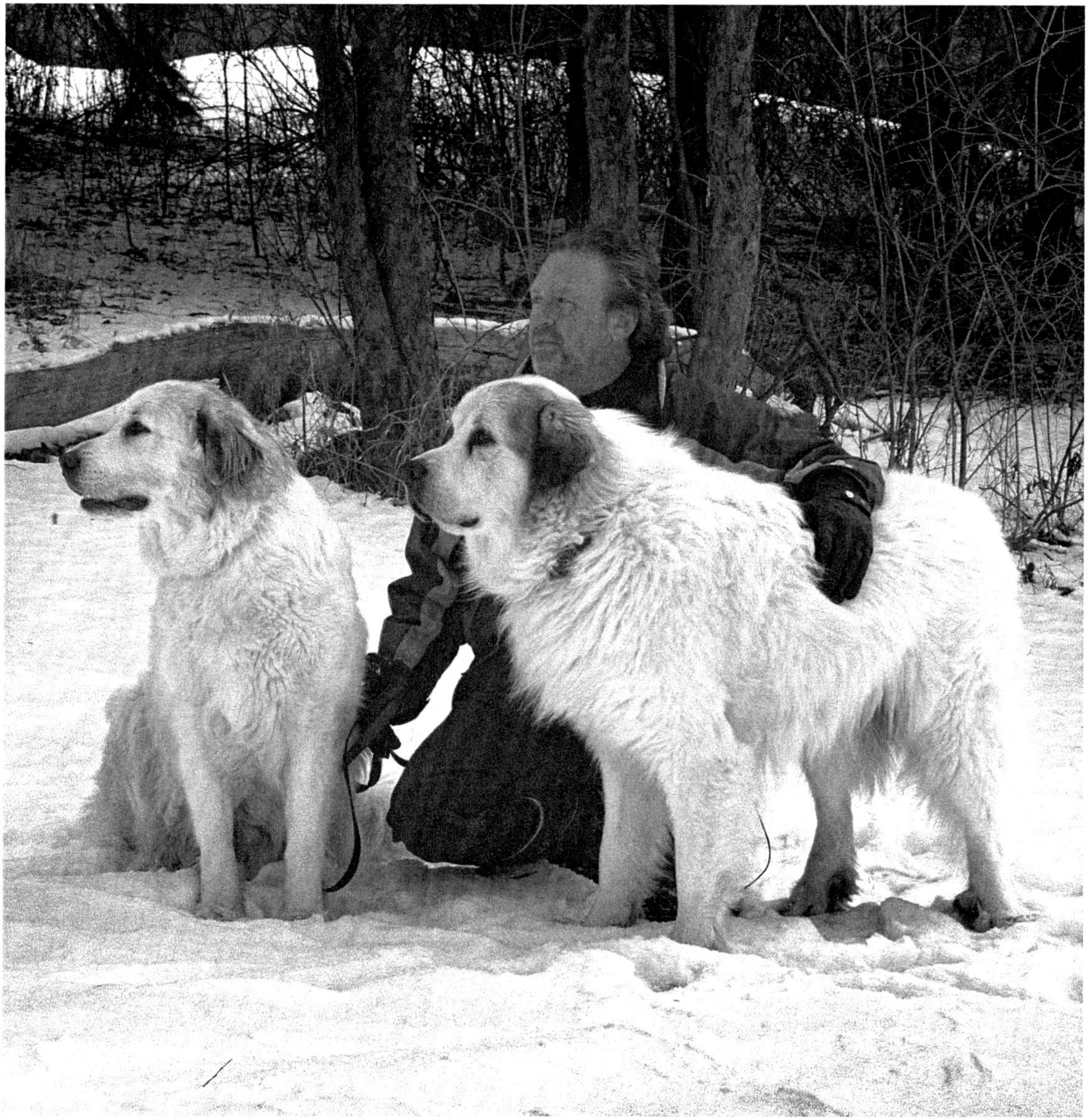

18 months and six homes later,
Paddington has found his forever home.

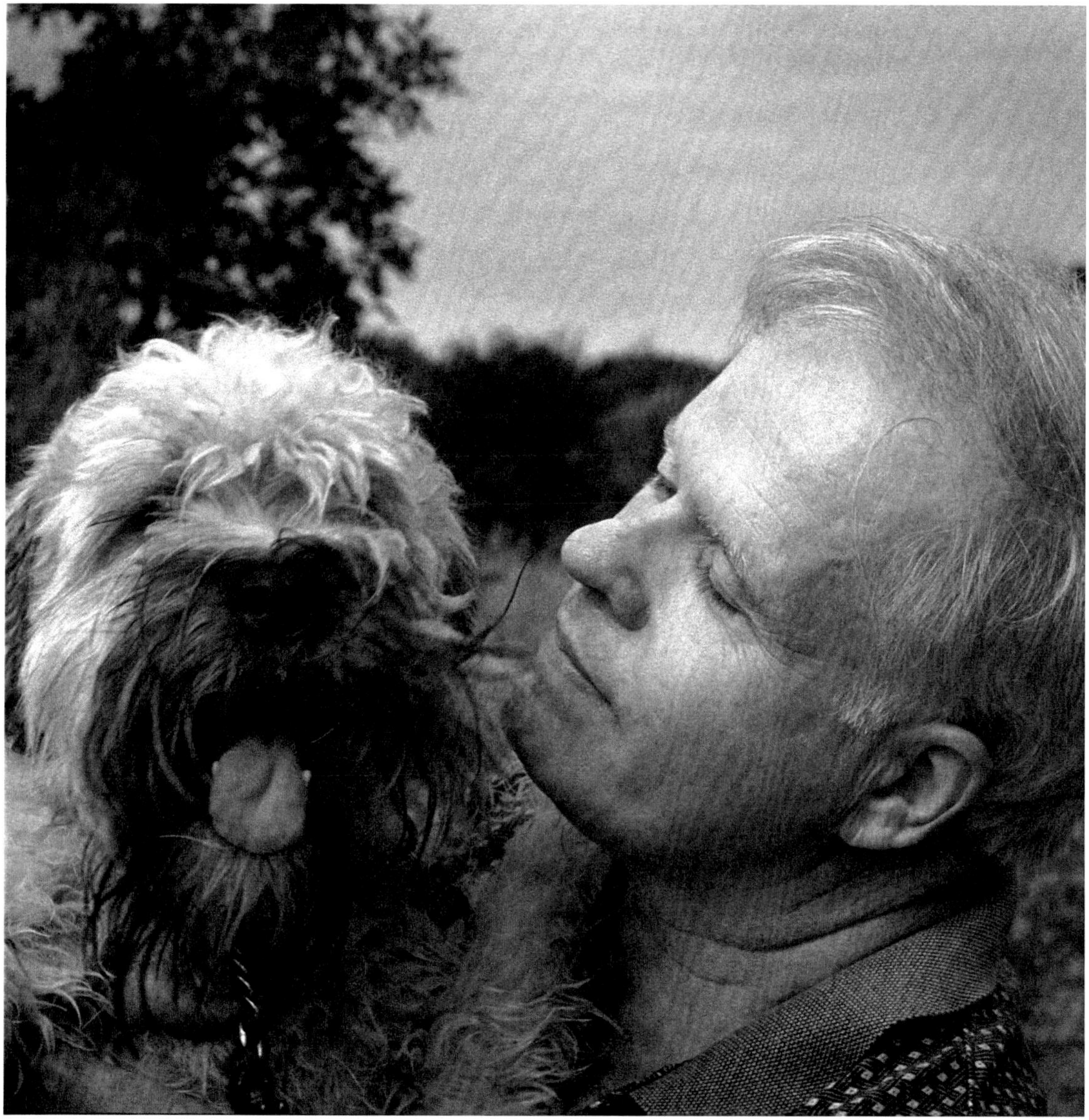

We were told Candle was 'active,'
tended to be 'strong-willed'
and could be a 'handful'.
We share so many traits –
no wonder we bonded so easily!

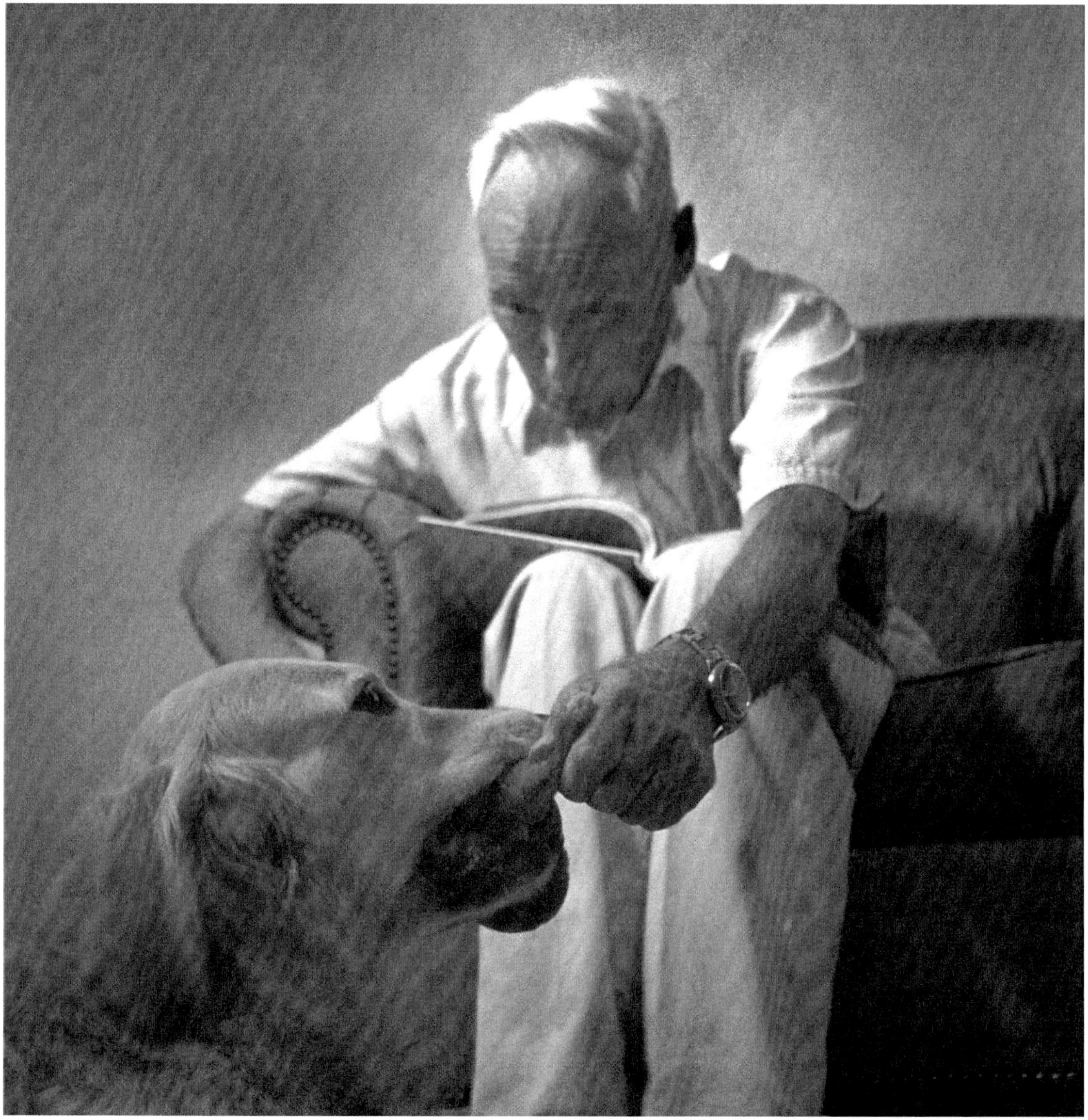

True happiness is simple:
a quiet moment of reflection
with a good friend.

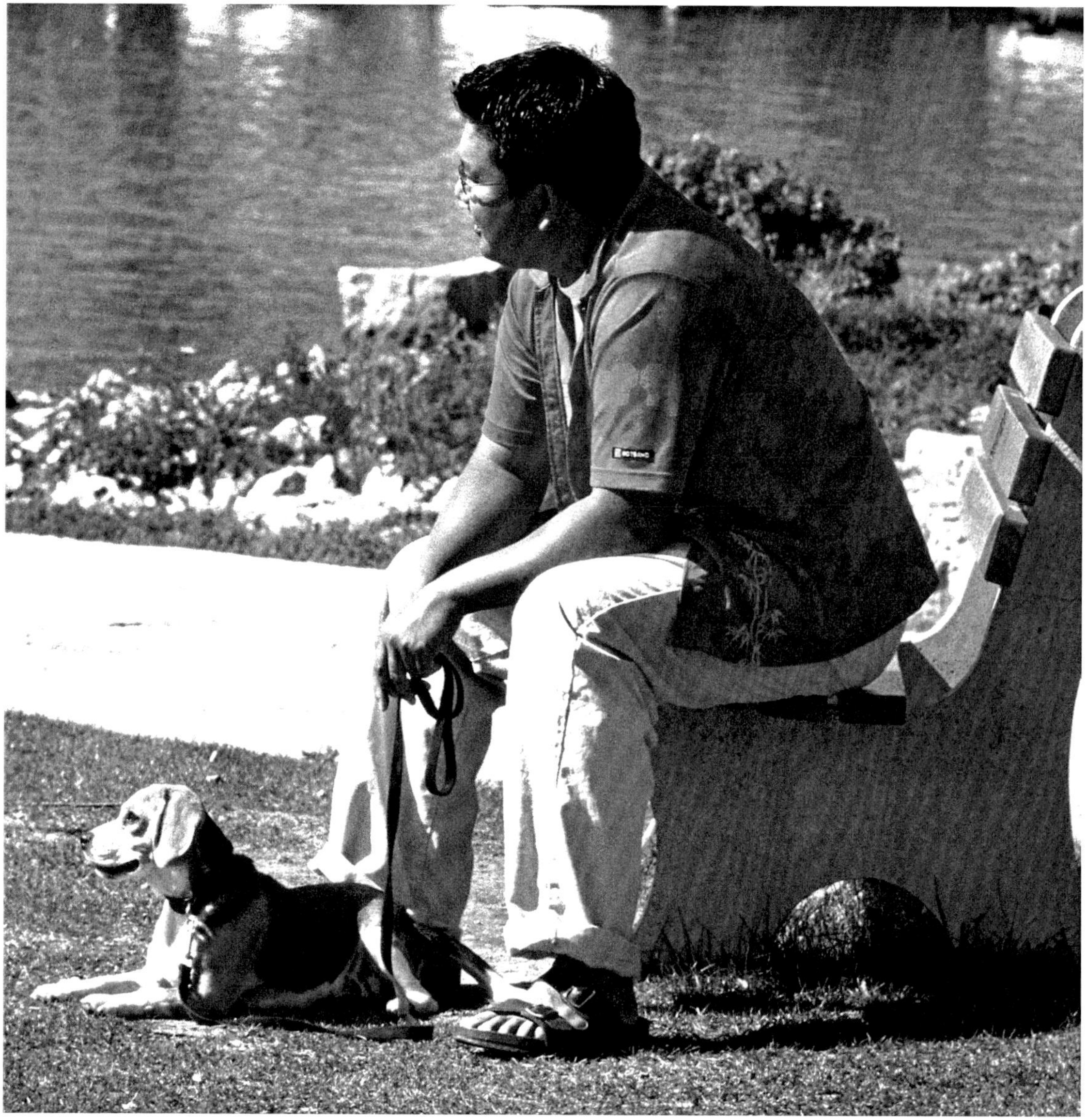

Happiness comes in threes.

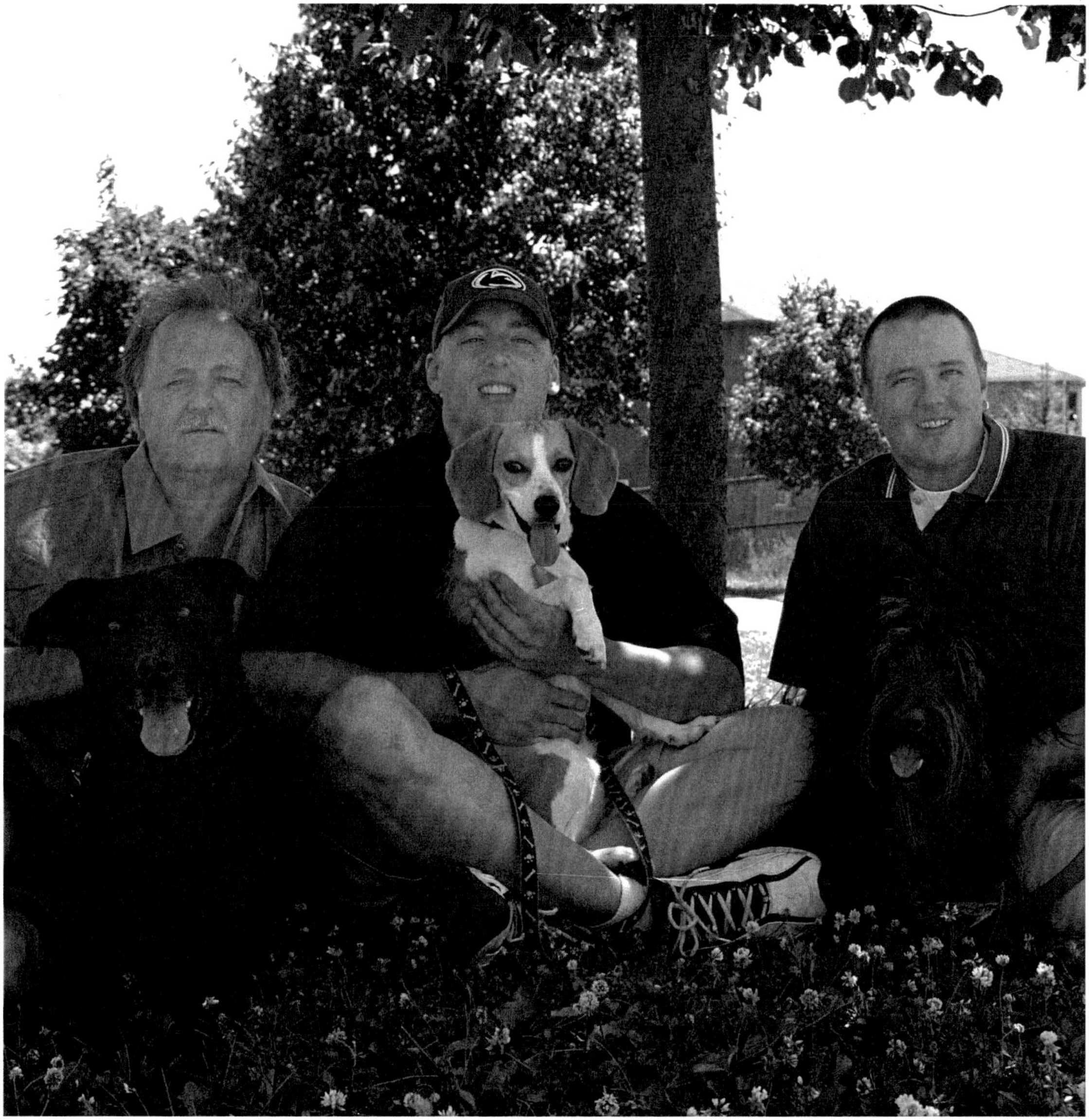

Each day begins
with a paw on the shoulder,
lots of kisses and tail wags,
and ends with paws and arms
entwined in contentment.

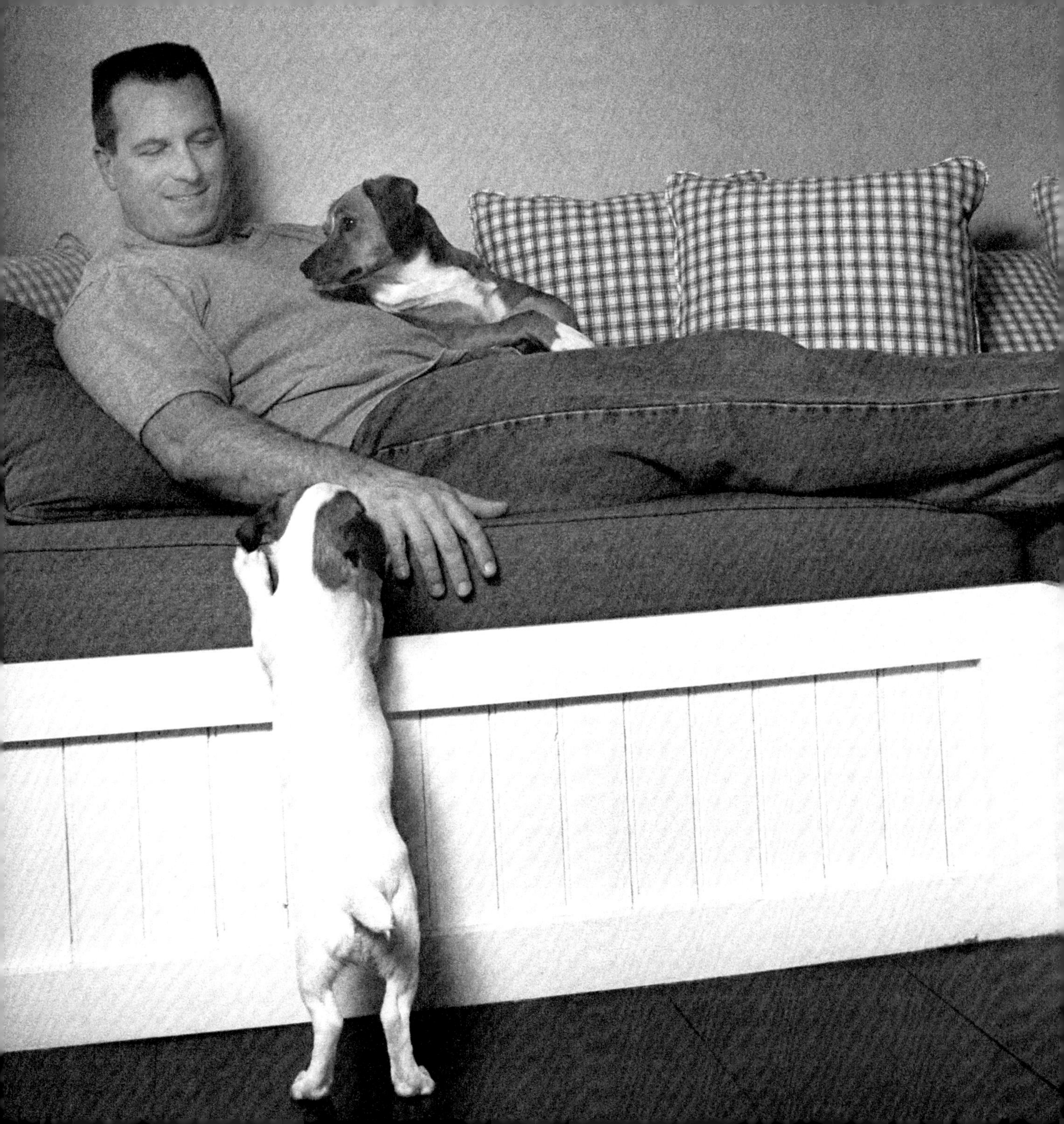

Our source of great joy is simple:
a walk to the park
followed by a chase around the house
with a squeaky toy.

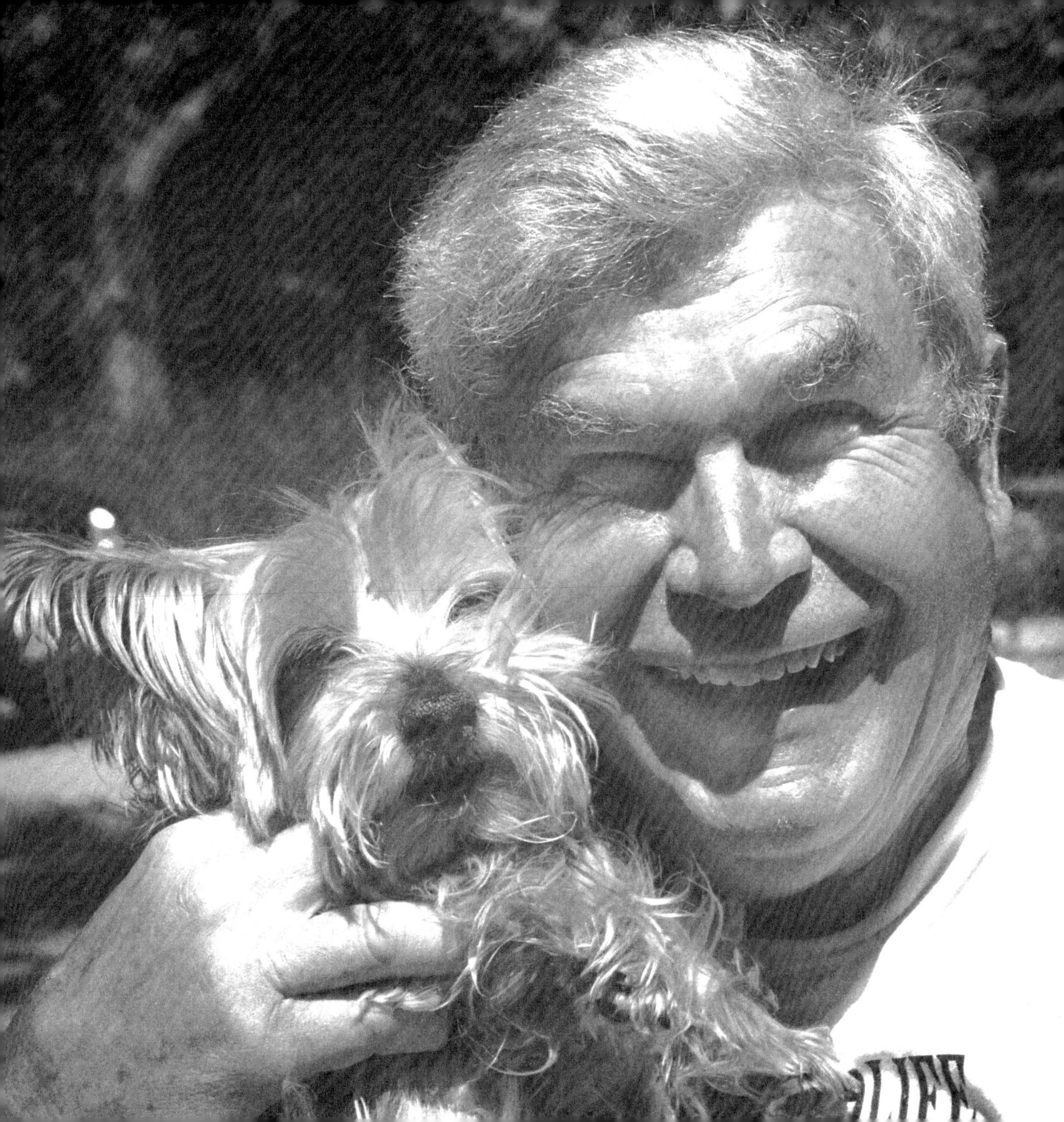

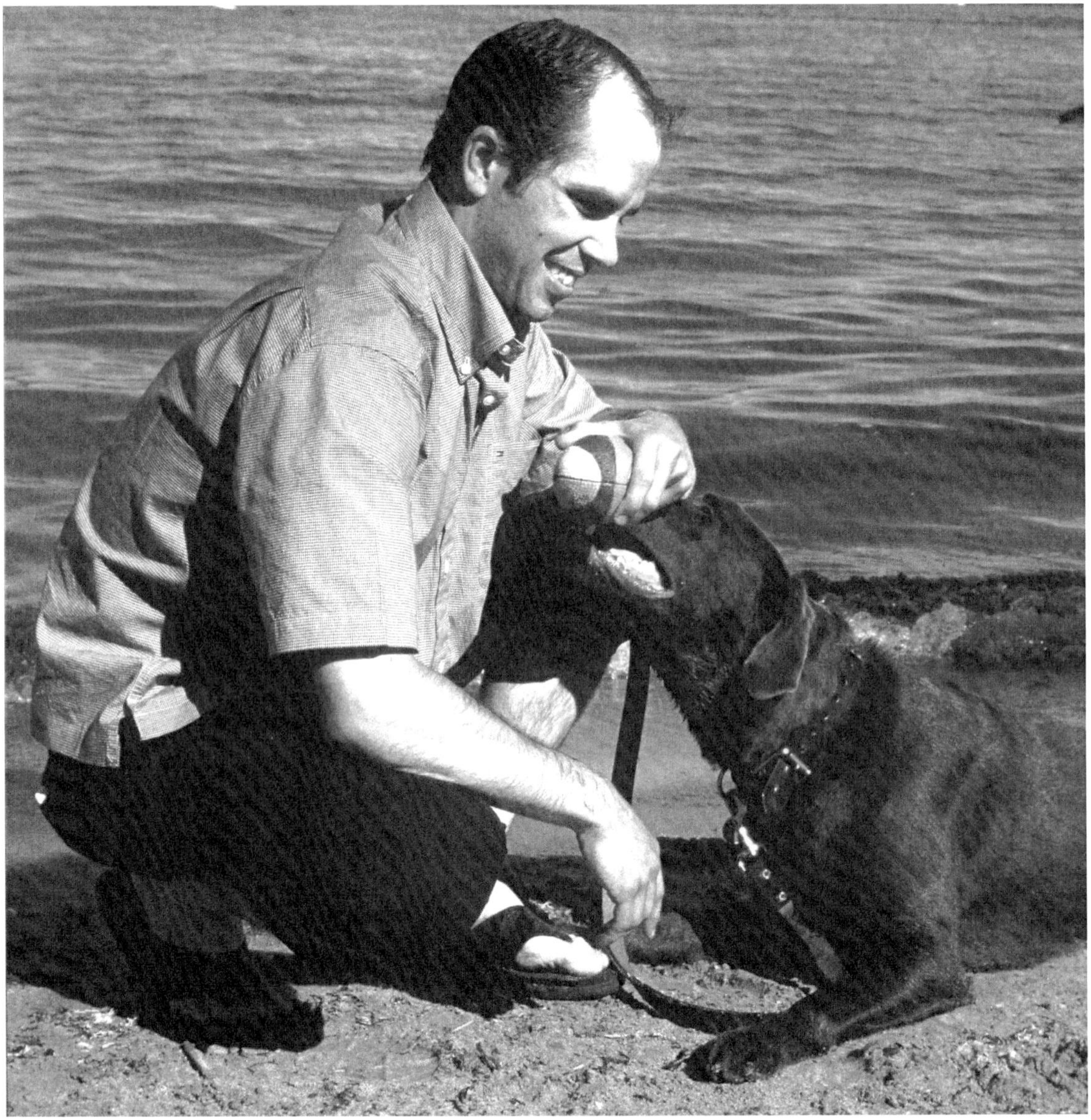

If he sees a body of water,
of any size,
he sets his sights on it,
but first looks to me for permission
before bounding off in pure pleasure.

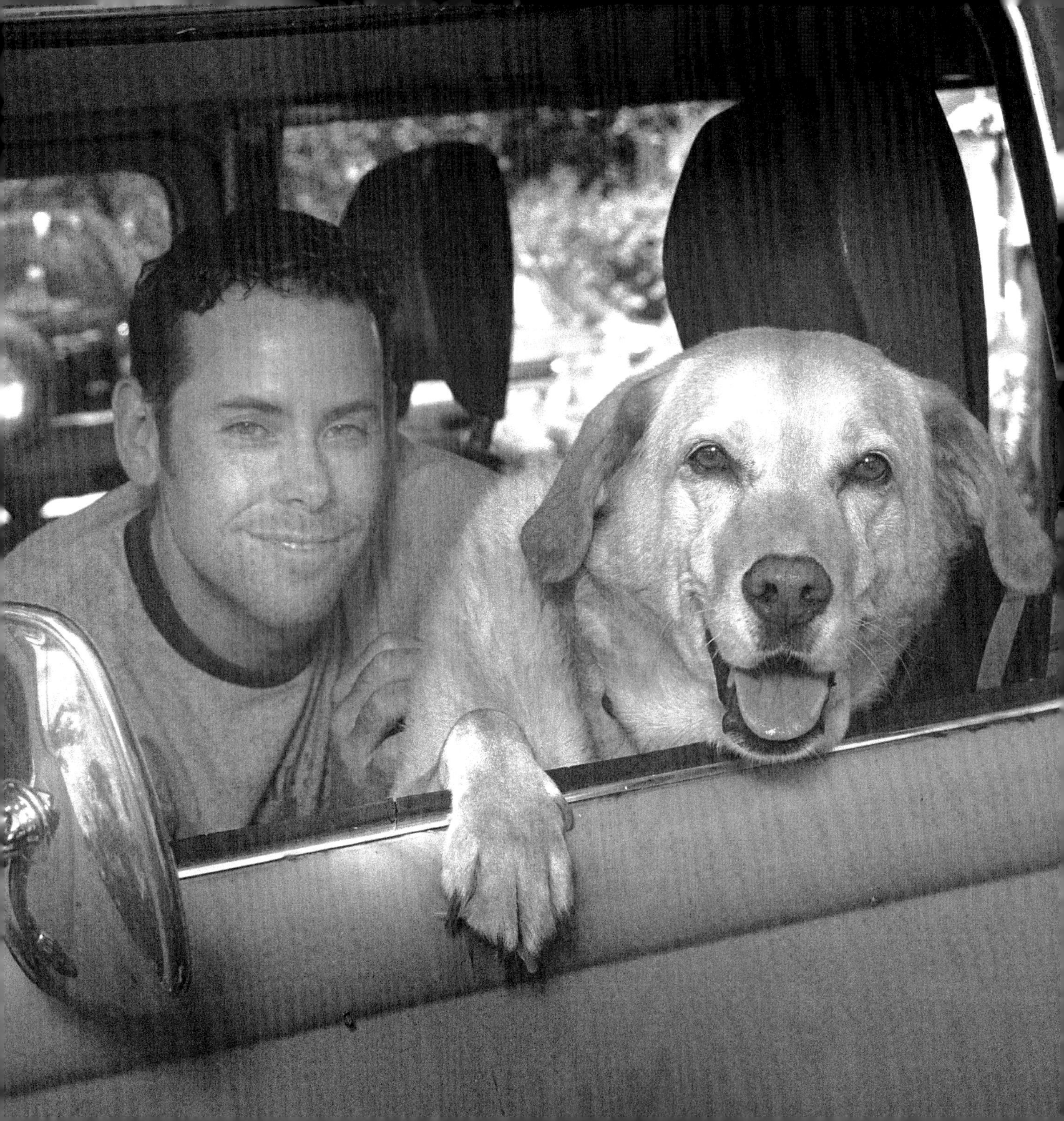

God may be some people's co-pilot,
however, I prefer Madison
who has yet to lead me astray.

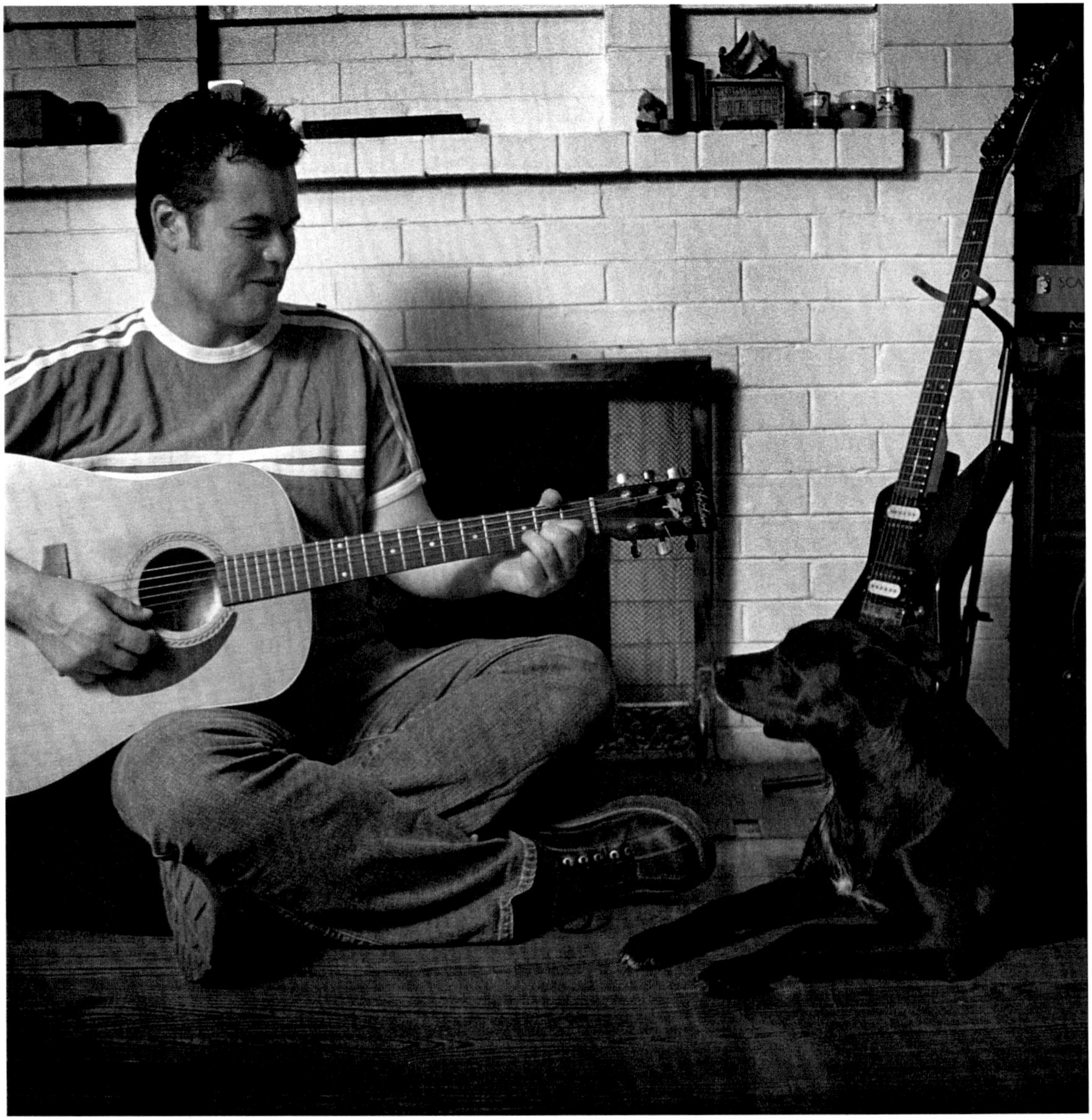

Music charms the savage beast.

Curiosity is for the young.
Contentment is for those
who have been around the block
a few times.

Seeing her energy and joy
with something as simple as a Frisbee
is very relaxing for me.

He may be a trained hunting dog,
but he is definitely more interested
in keeping chipmunks and squirrels
on their toes than retrieving fallen prey.

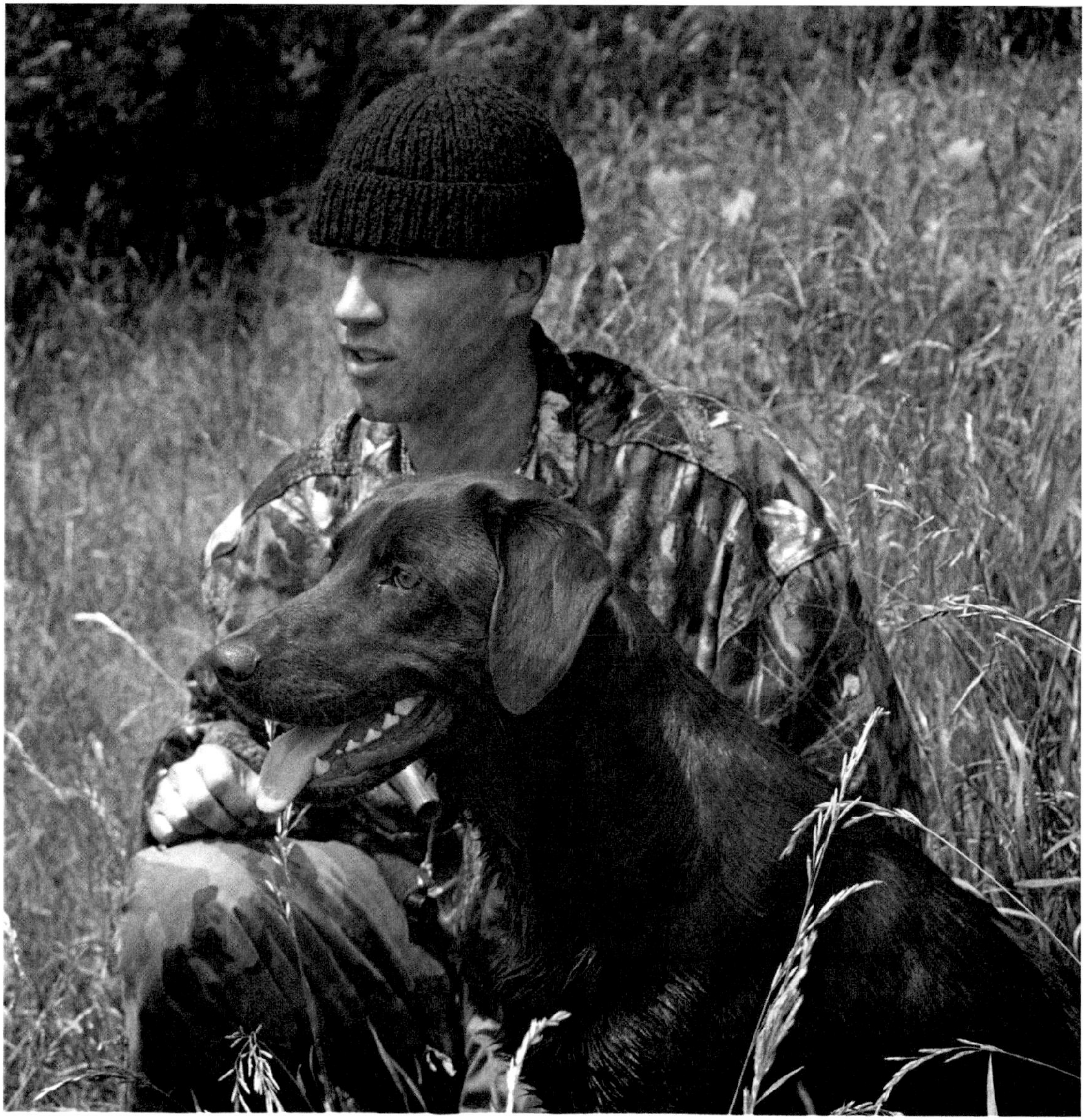

I'm the one he mooches dinner from.

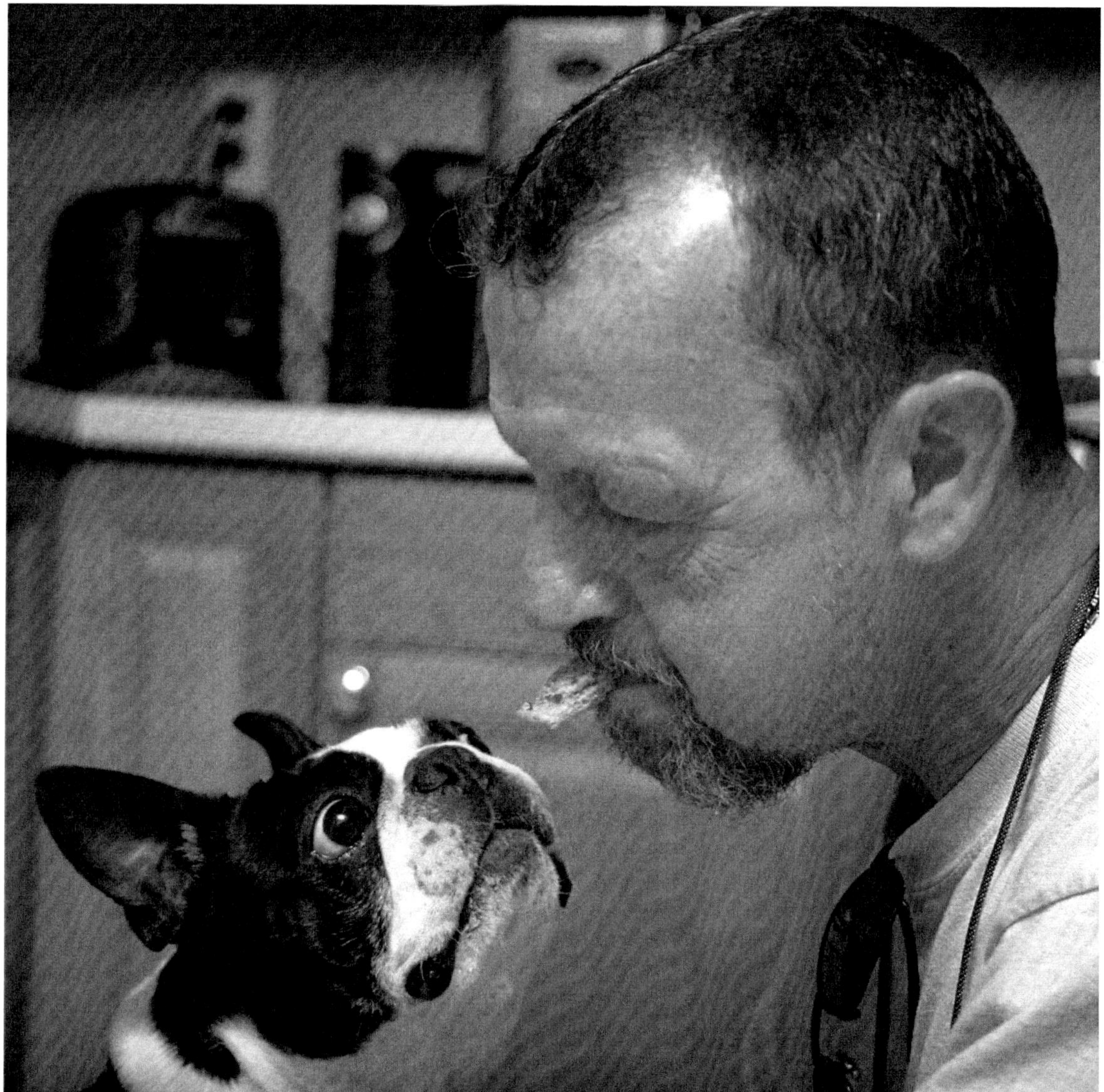

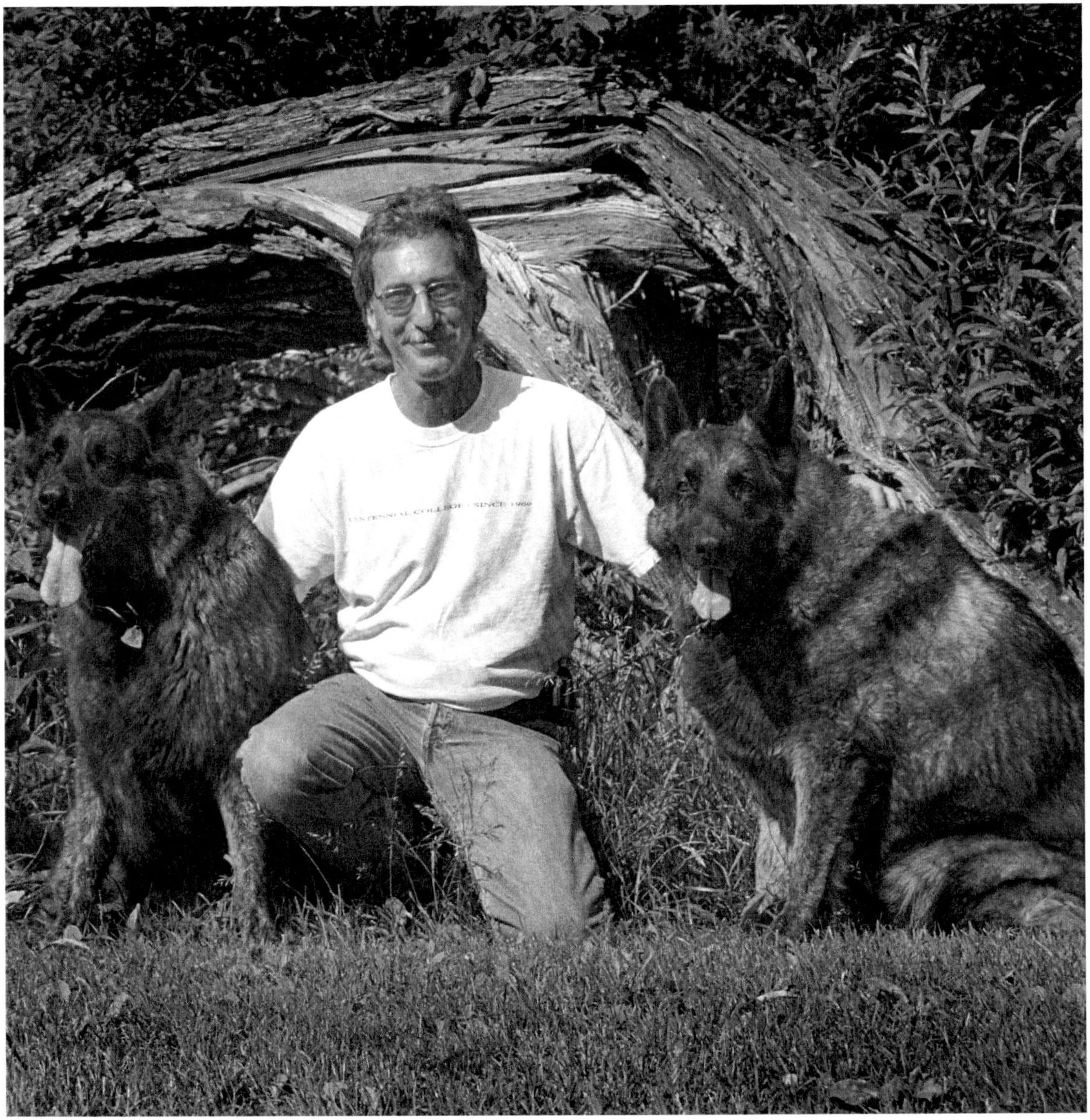

My boys love to play fetch,
but they don't have it quite right:
they know how to fetch the ball,
they just don't know how to return it.

Having Rory makes stressful days
at the office ancient history
with just one wag of the tail.
She's more than just a best friend,
she's my therapist.

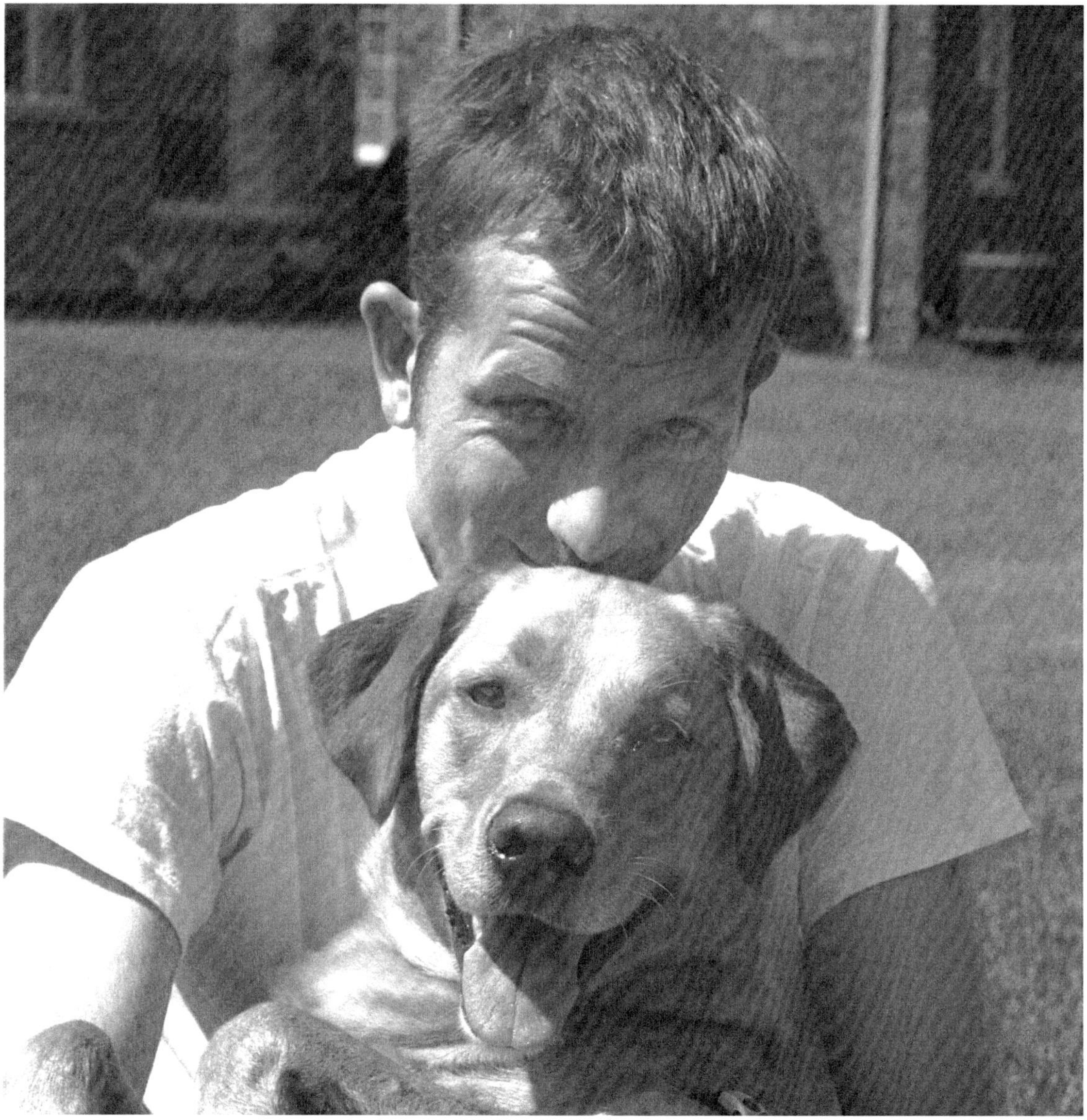

Rain, snow or sun,
a day with Hank
is a day well spent.

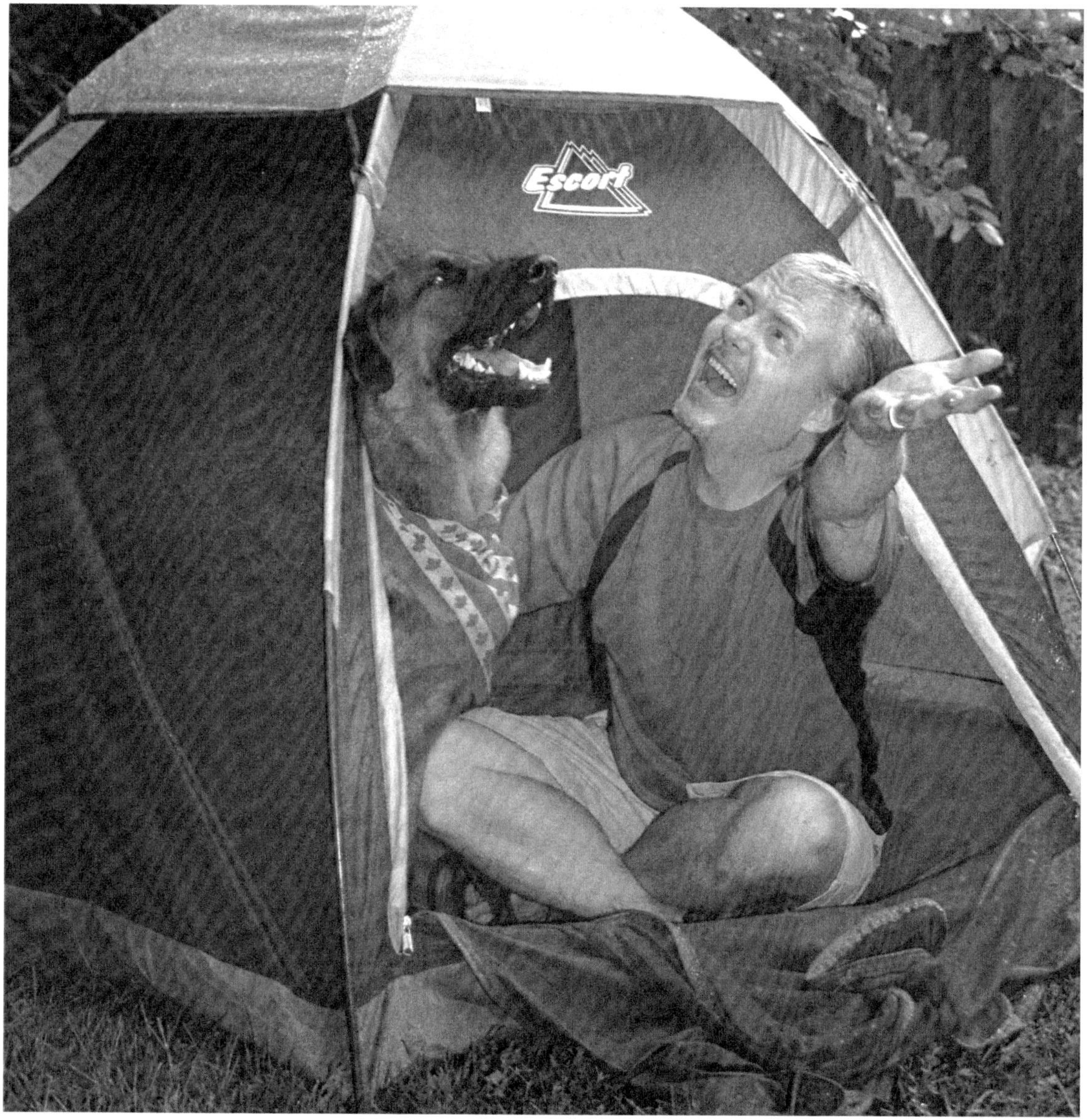
Escort

Who's turn is it to drive?

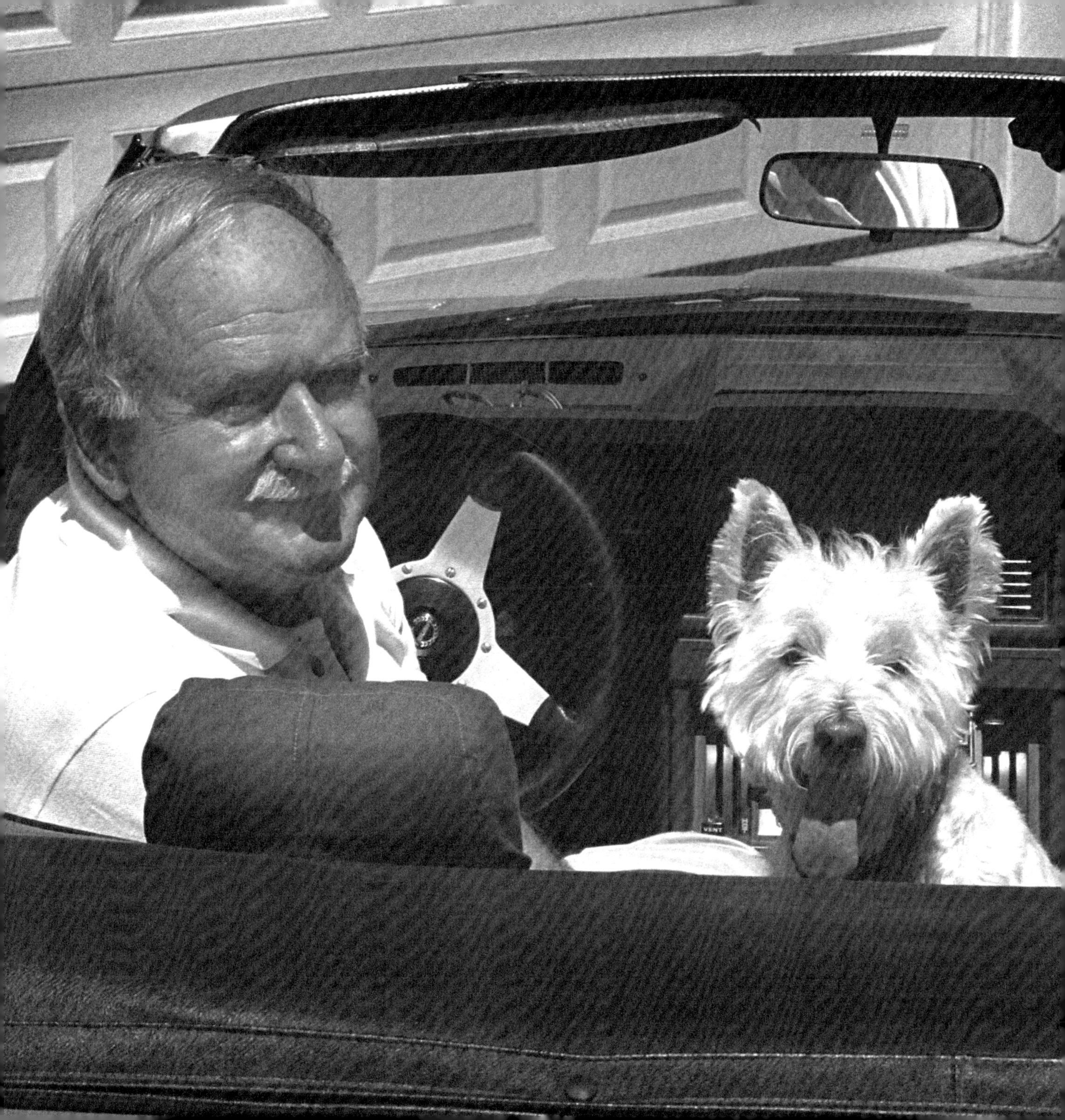

A second opinion
from someone
with a superior sense of smell
is always welcome.

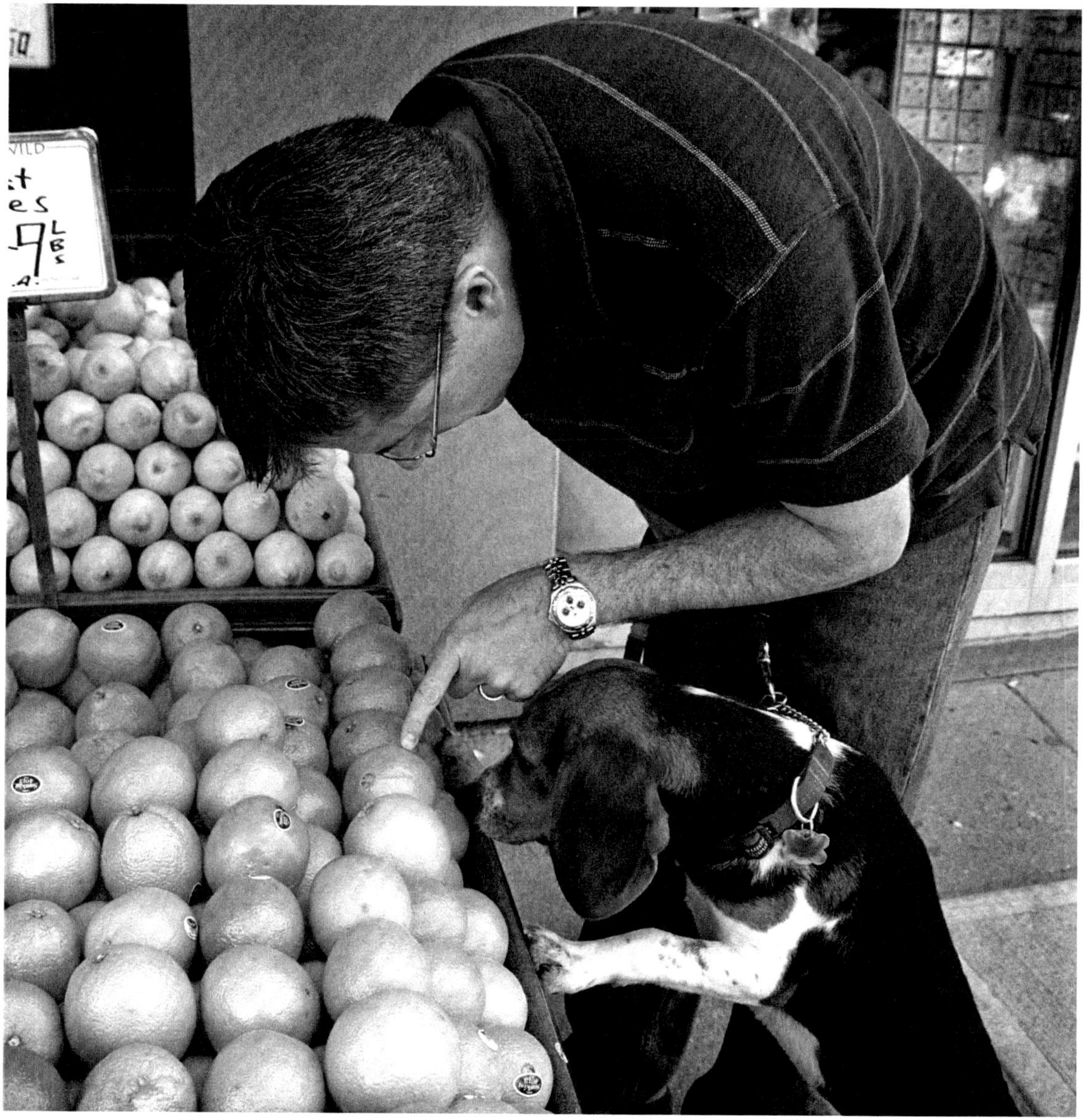

With his help,
the simplest job on the farm
can be done in only twice the time.

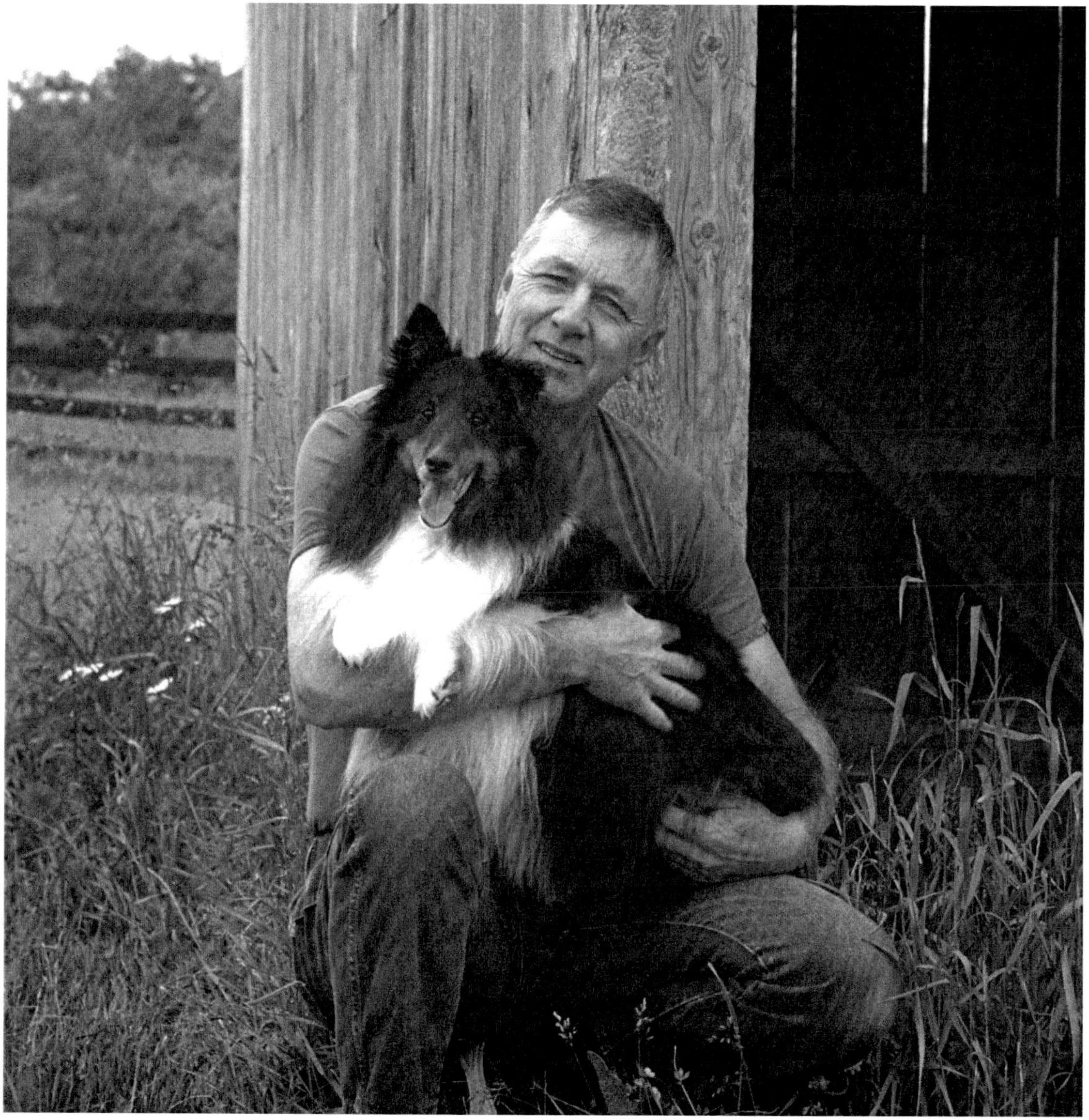

The family that swims together,
stays together.

Inspiration for greatness comes in all forms.
The best inspiration has fur,
a wet nose
and a tail that won't quit.

Only dogs can make me chuckle
simply by being themselves.

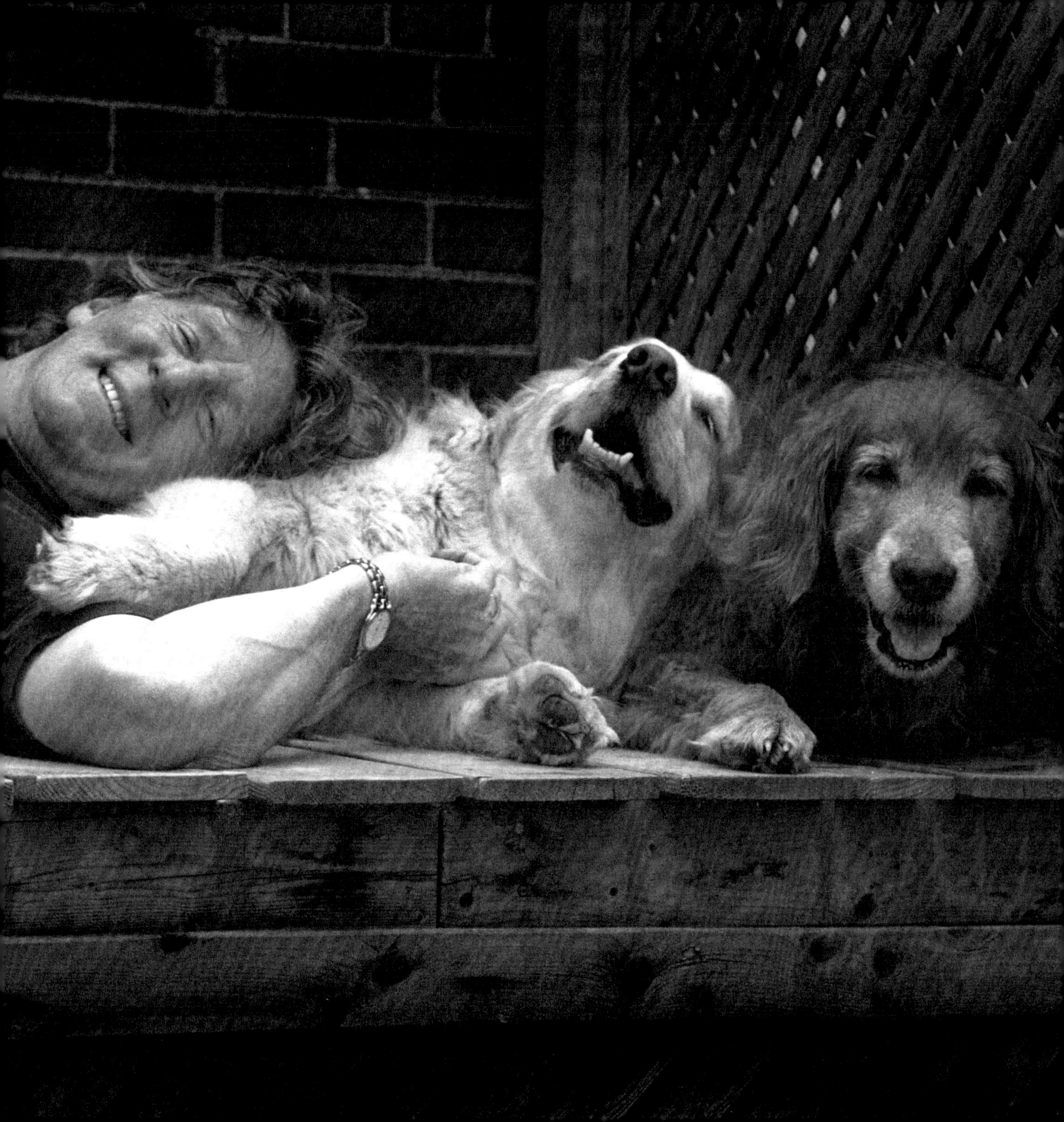

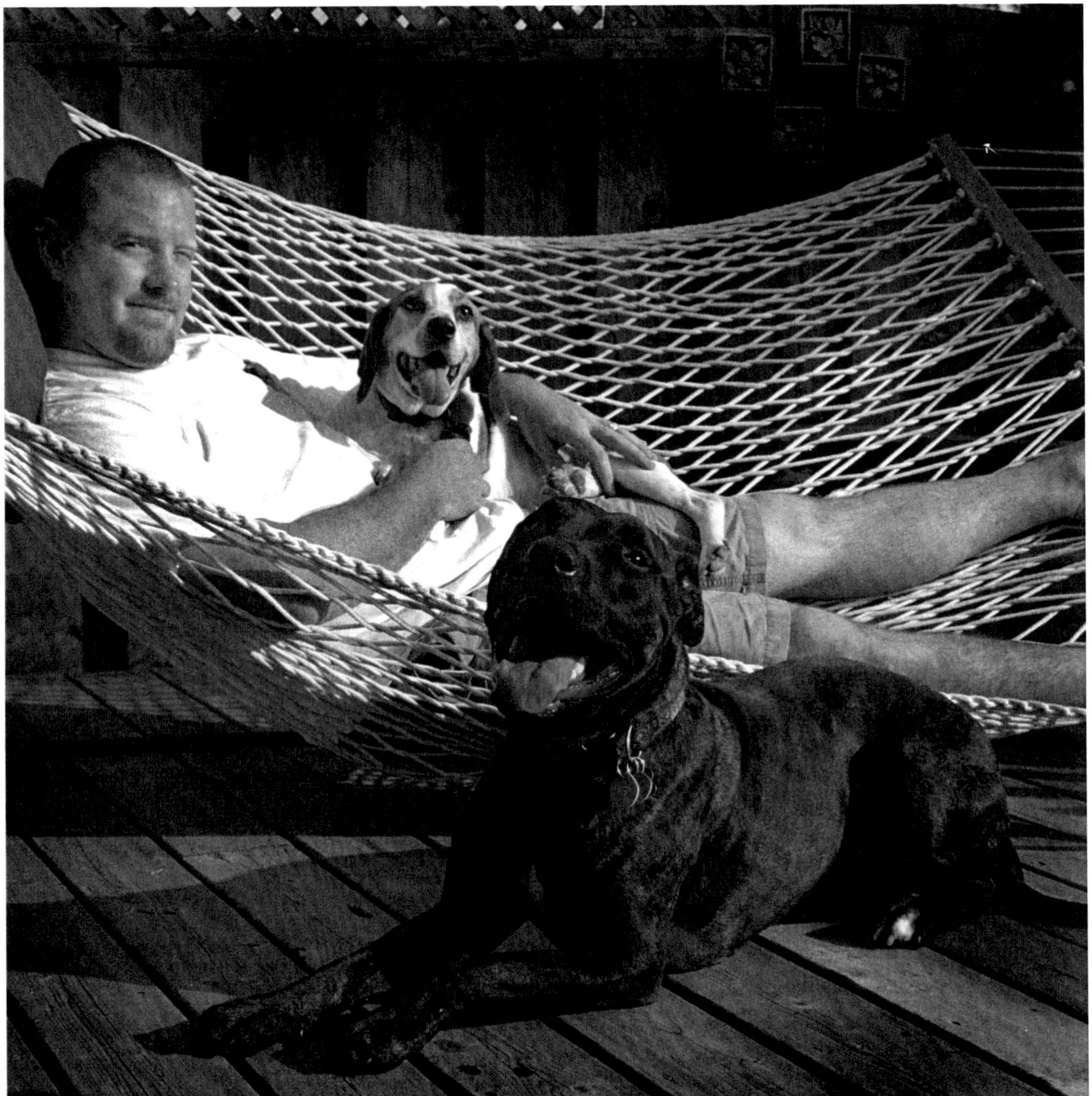

Look up the word 'content' in the dictionary
and you'll find a picture of
Nicky, Sebastian and me.

One look said it all:
'I'm staying with you.'

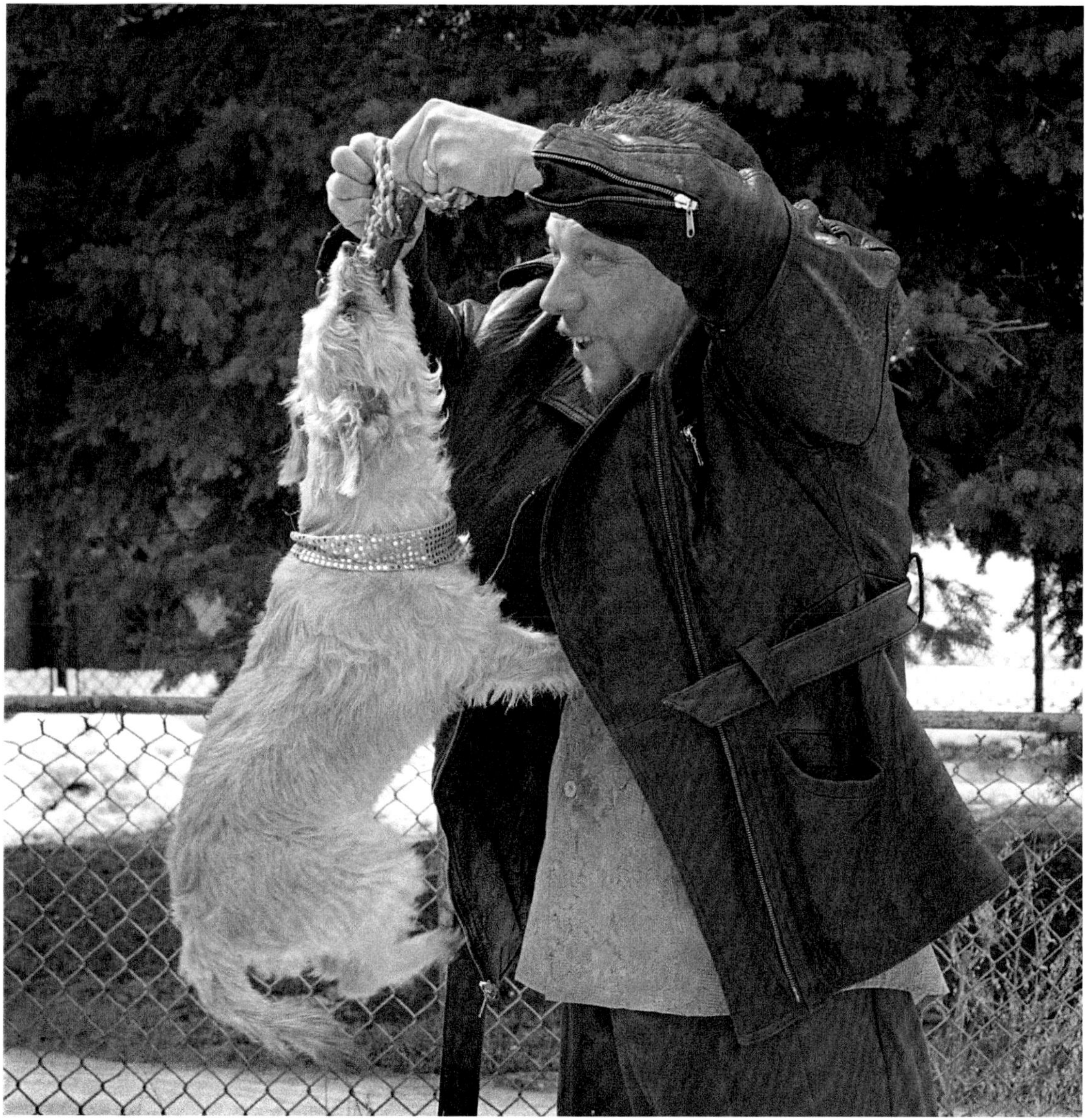

'Joey's Boxing Day Sale'
is the clown of all dogs
and the one that makes me
smile every day.

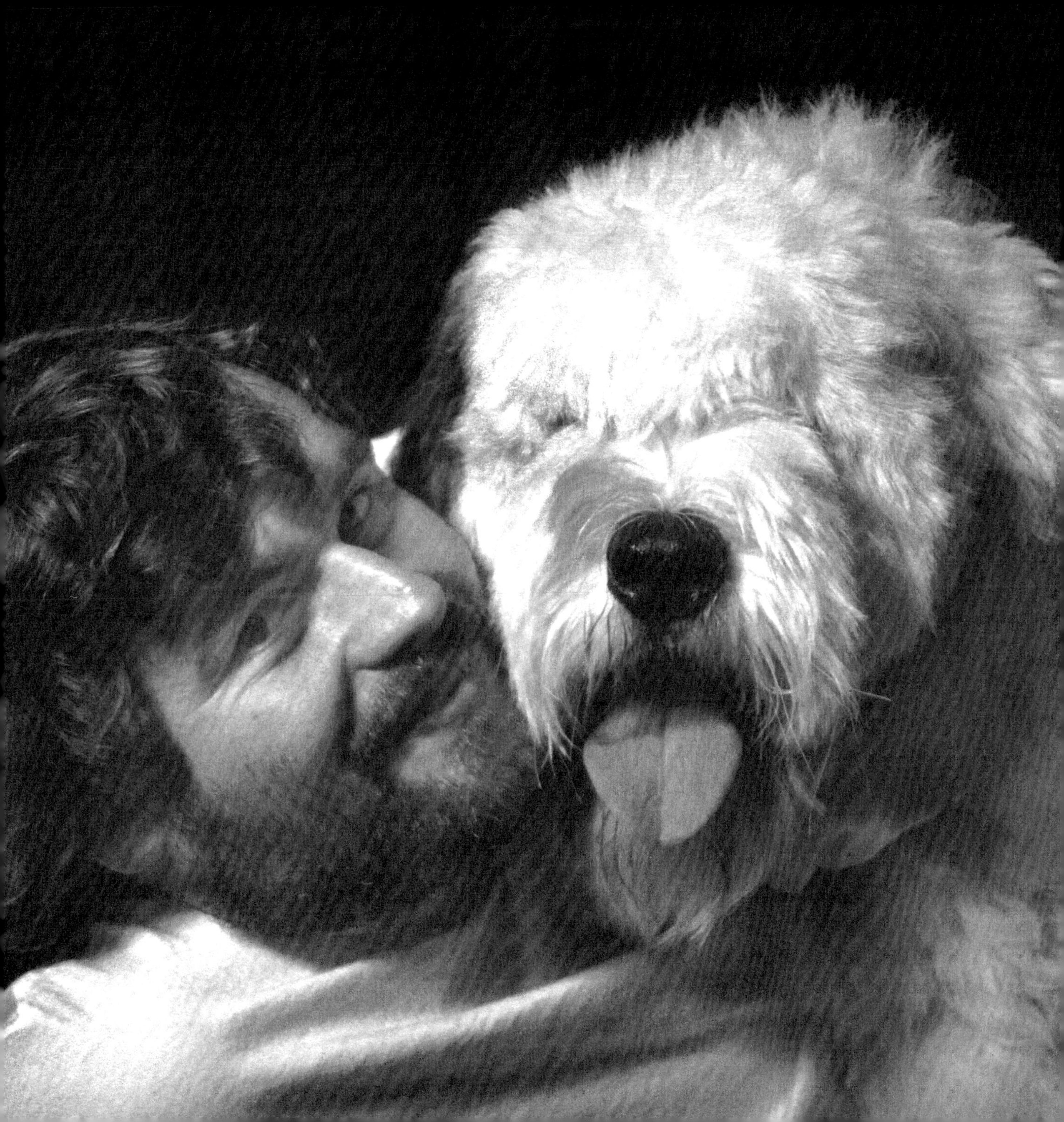

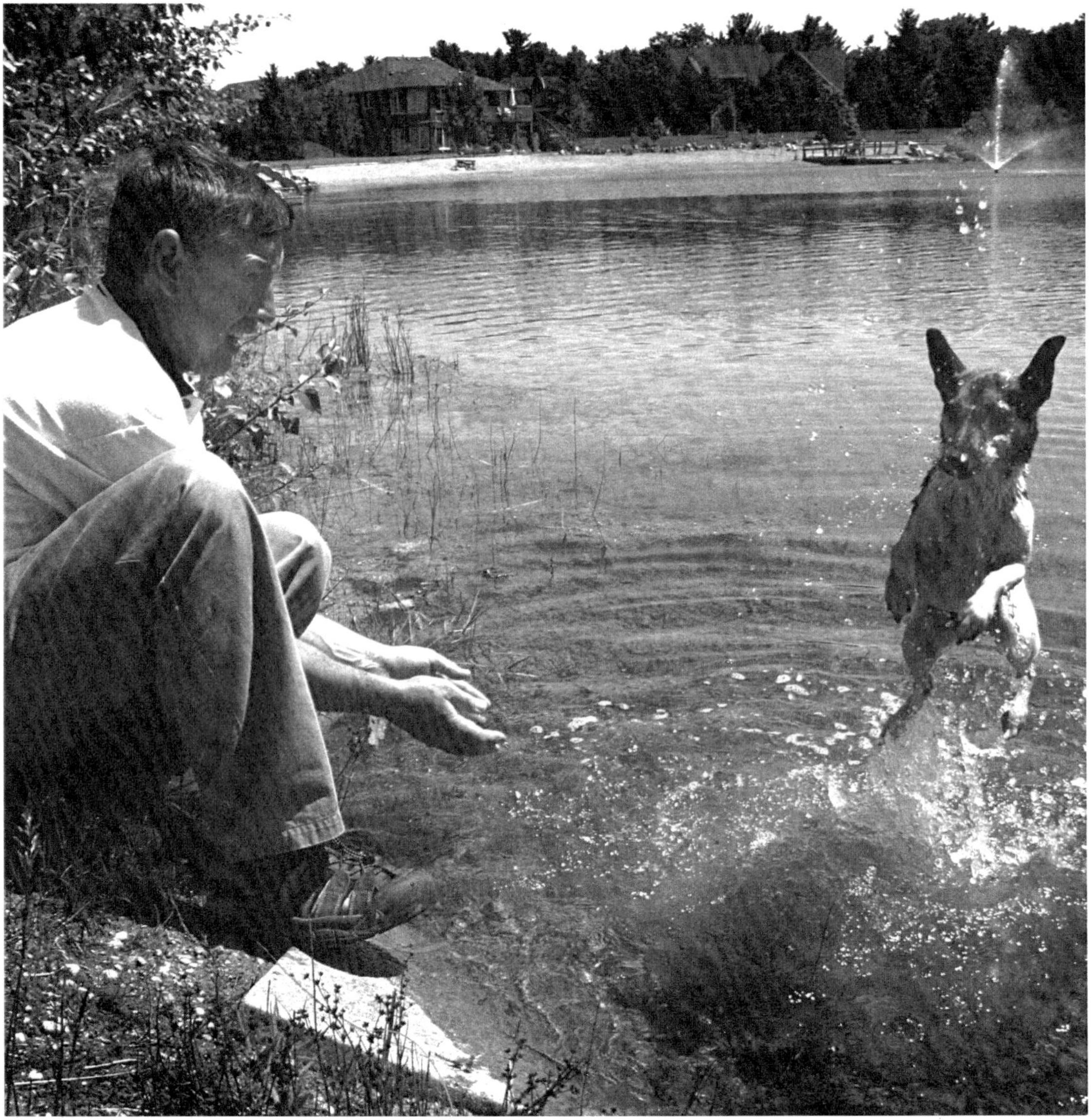

There's no other way to describe Britta:

joie de vivre!

Winston and I are taking obedience classes together.
I have become very obedient.

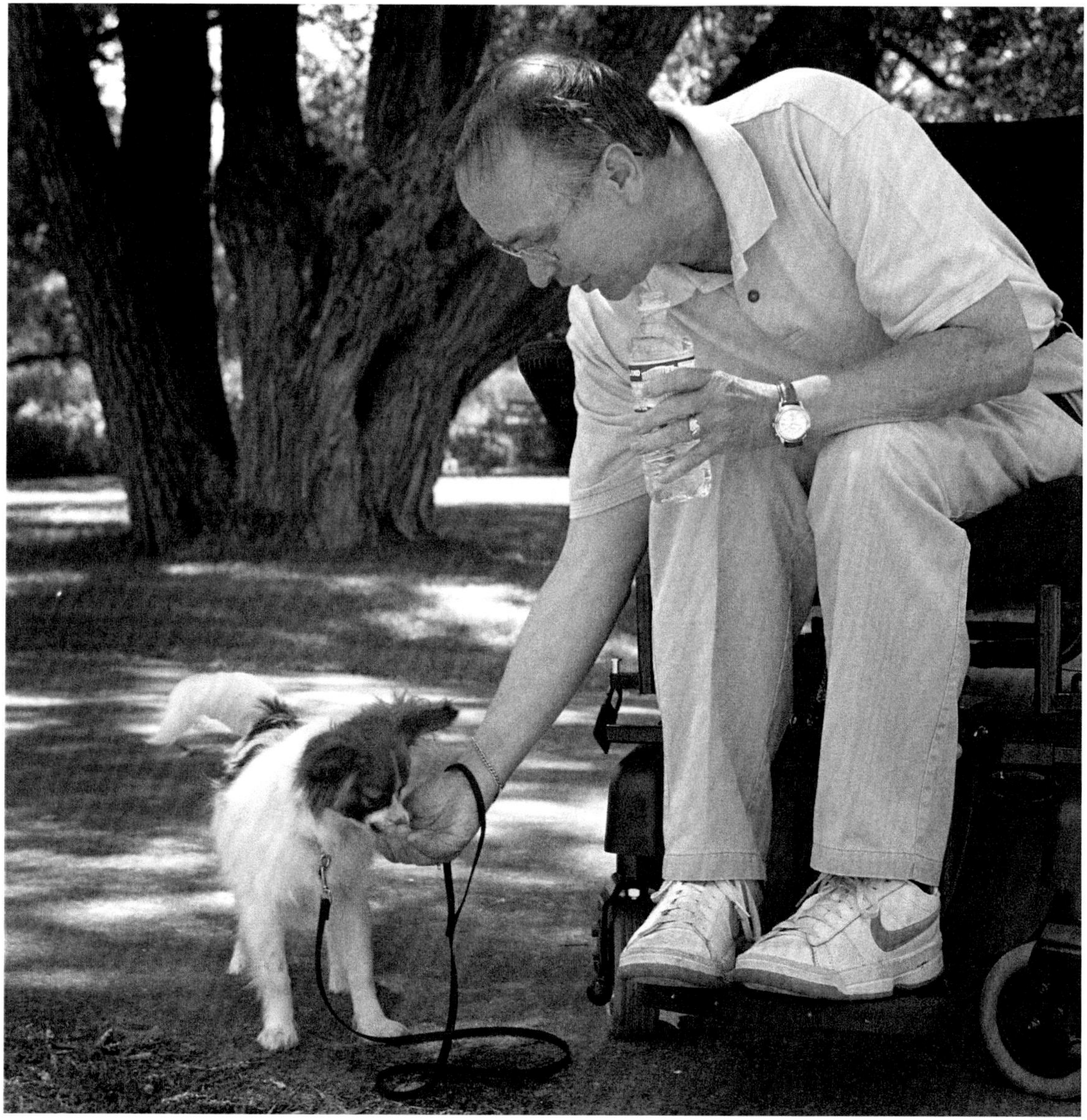

Beware the tug of a Bulldog -
it's often a yank
on the heartstrings.

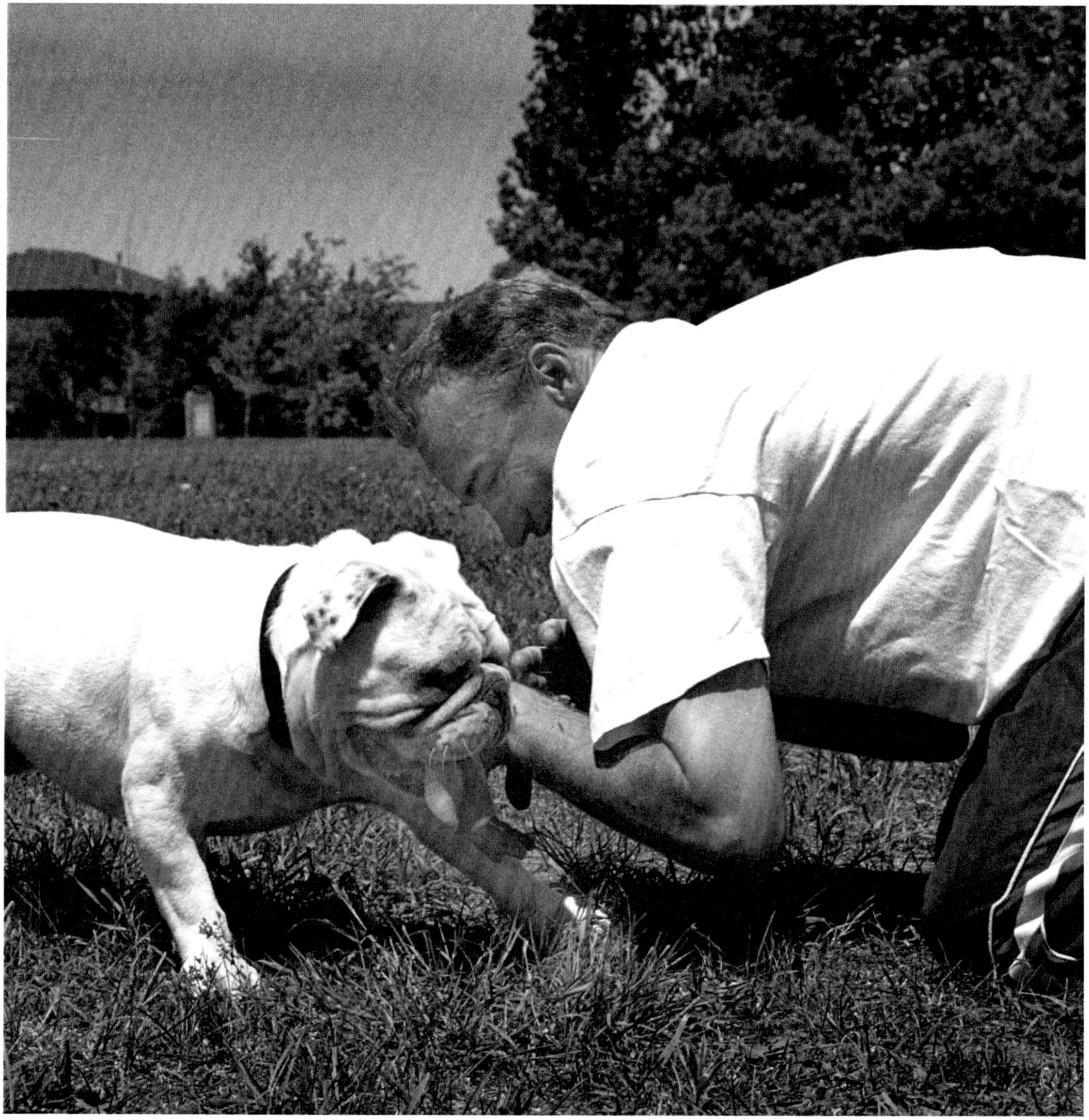

The food in someone else's bowl is always better.

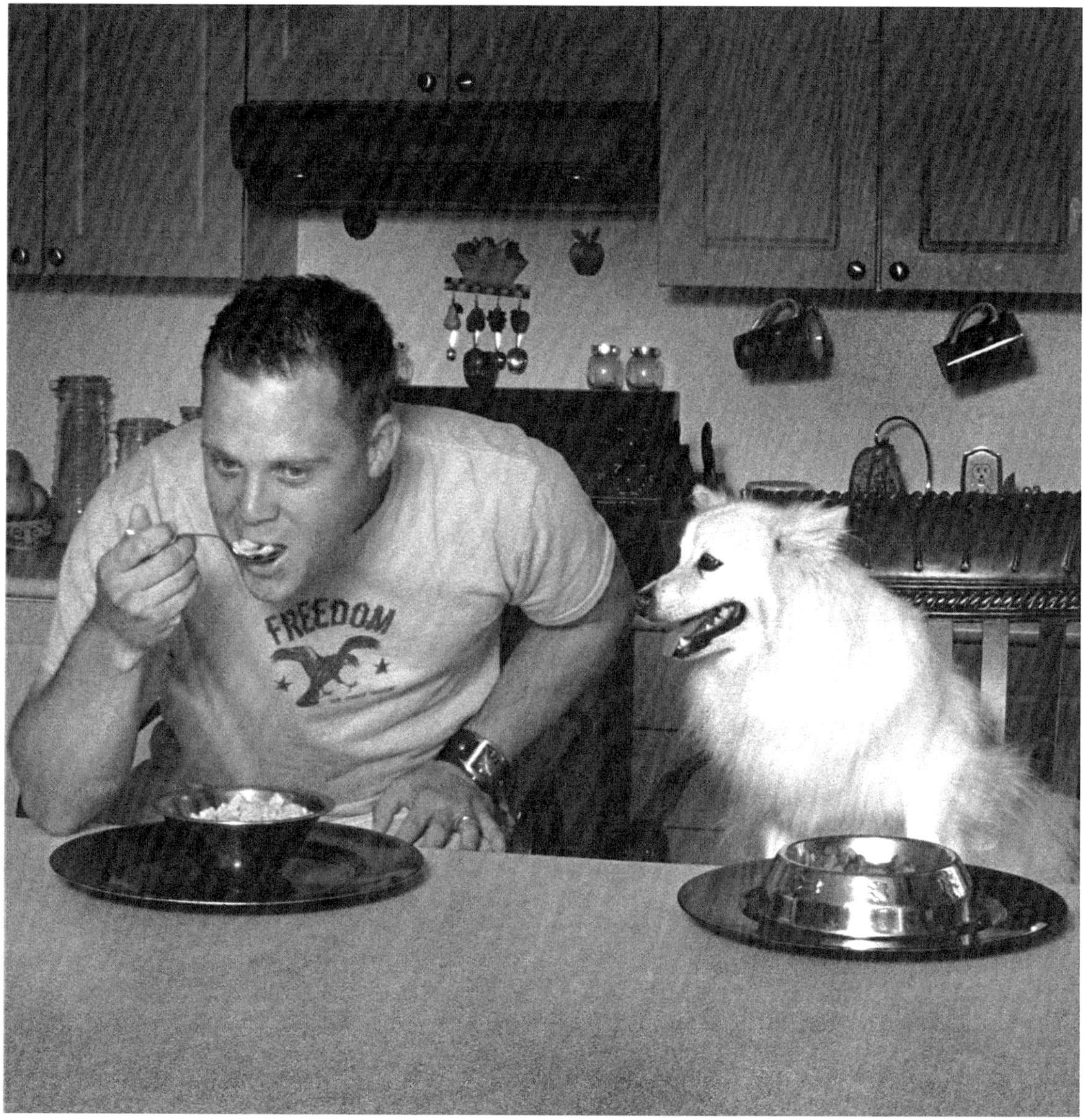
FREEDOM

My phone is screwed –
the puppies chewed it.
Love them dearly,
but I hate using a tin can and string
to make a call.

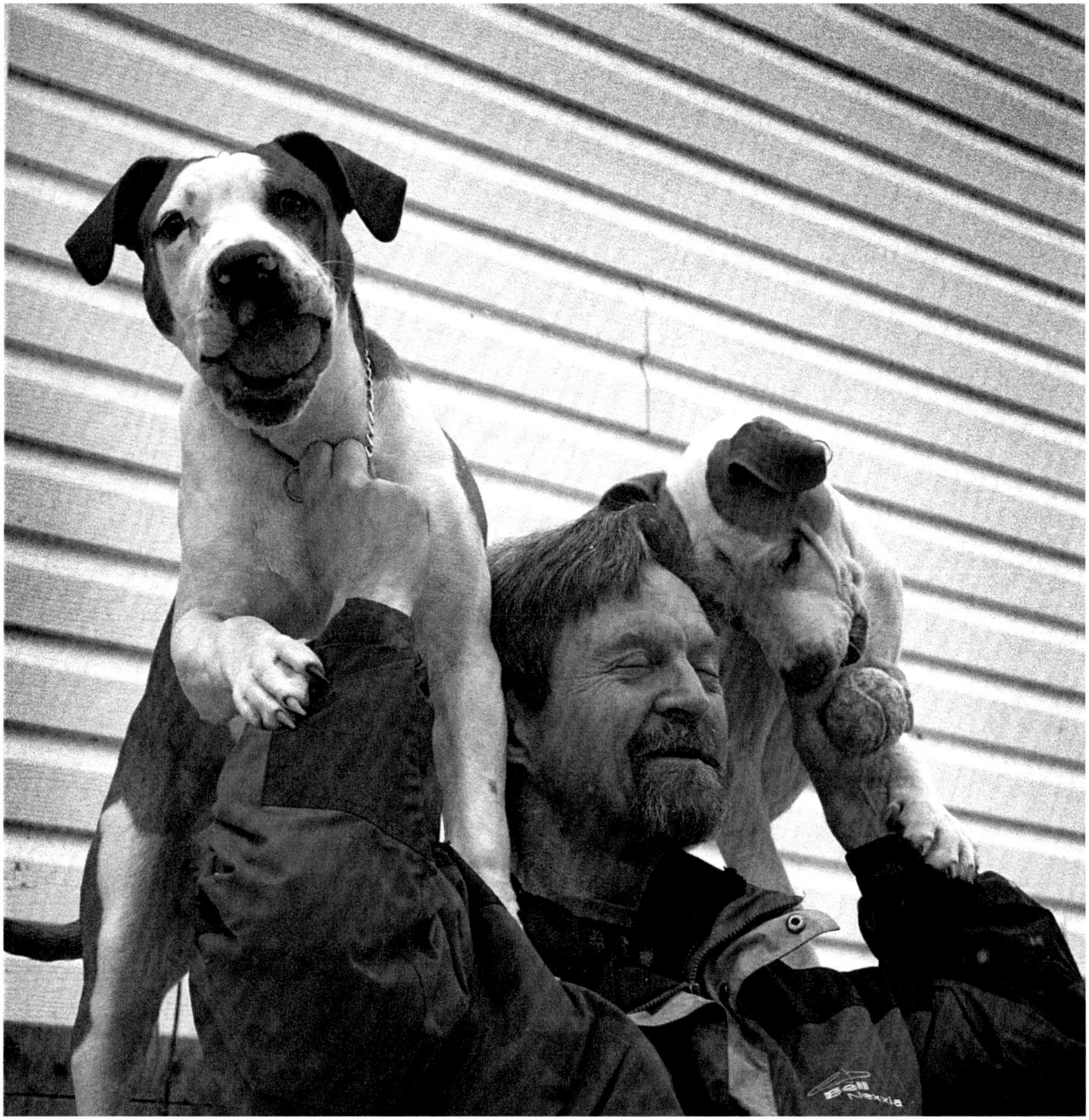
Bell Nexxia

I wasn't interested in owning a dog
and only agreed to Sally staying with us for a short time
to keep the peace with the wife.
Sally thought otherwise of the arrangement
and she is here to stay.

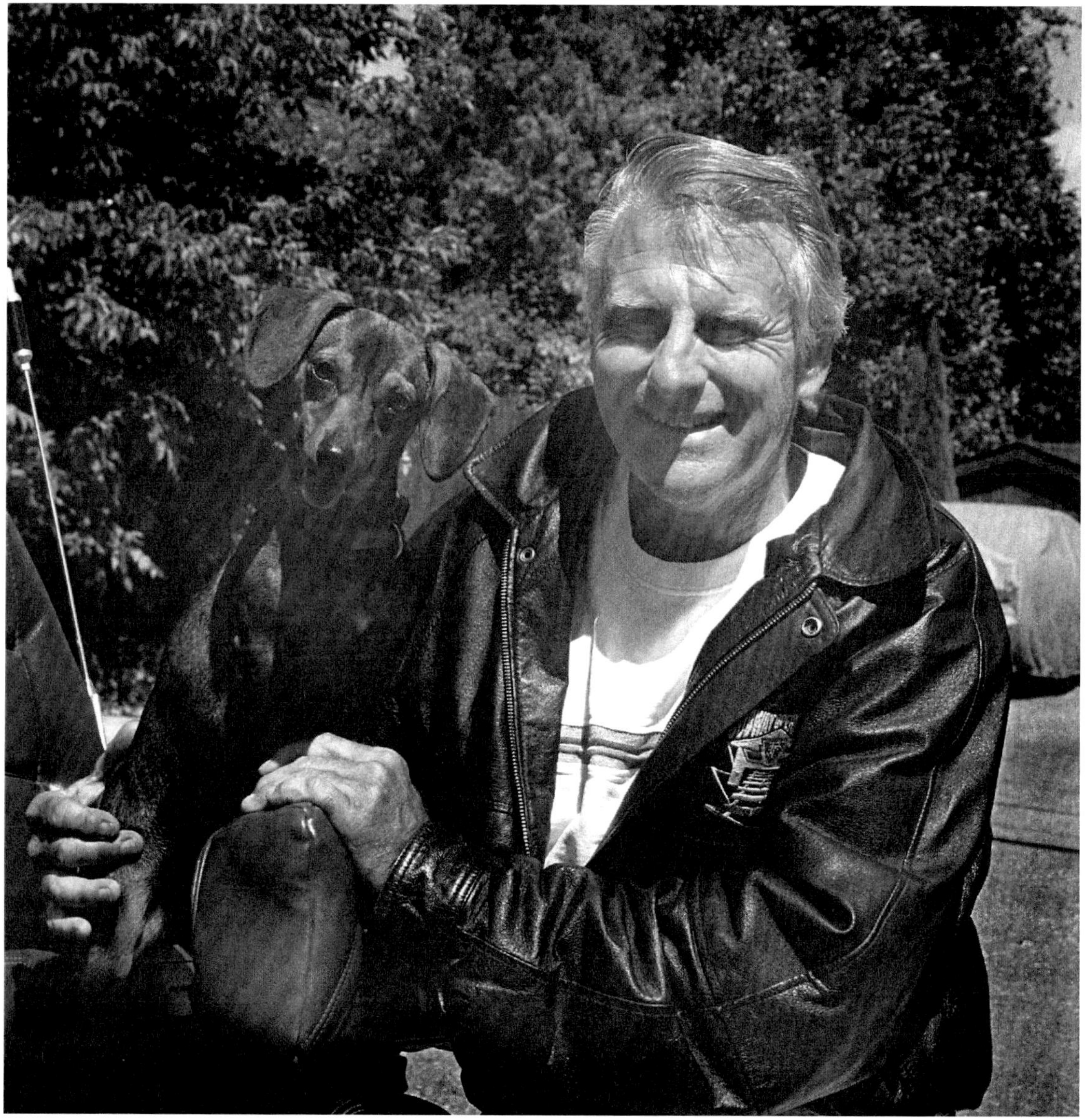

For true love,
just follow your nose.

ROCK
BIG BAND JAZZ
THE COMPLETE ELVIS
MESOAMERICA'S ANCIENT CITIES
CHEVROLET CAMARO '82 thru '90
HAYNES
CHEVROLET CHEVELLE
HAYNES

When I first laid eyes on them
they were dirty, matted, smelled bad,
was nervous and none-too-friendly or happy.
It just goes to show
you what a little TLC,
and a good bath, can do.

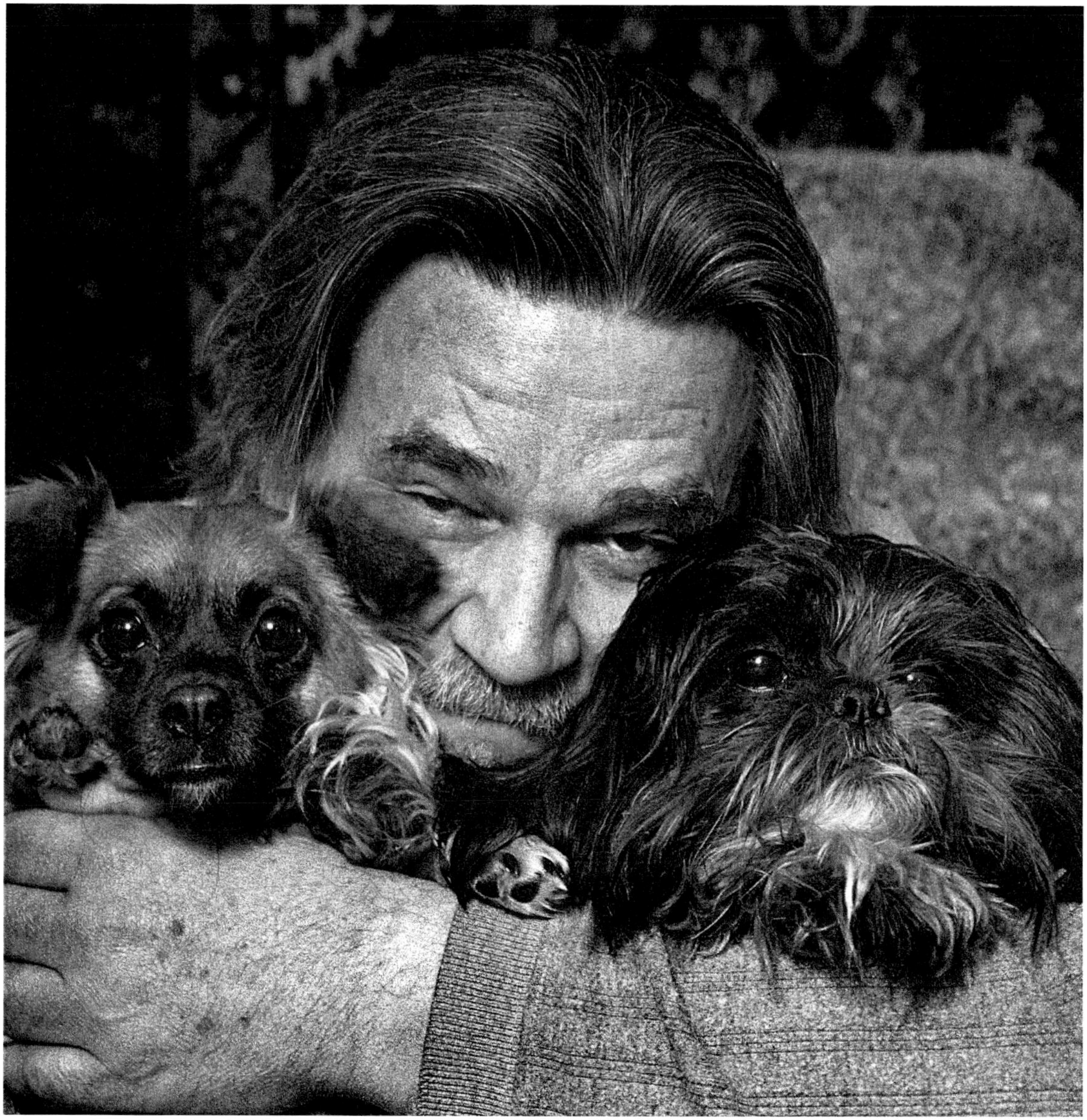

Each day is a 'groundhog'
type of day
where all is forgotten
and a new day begins.

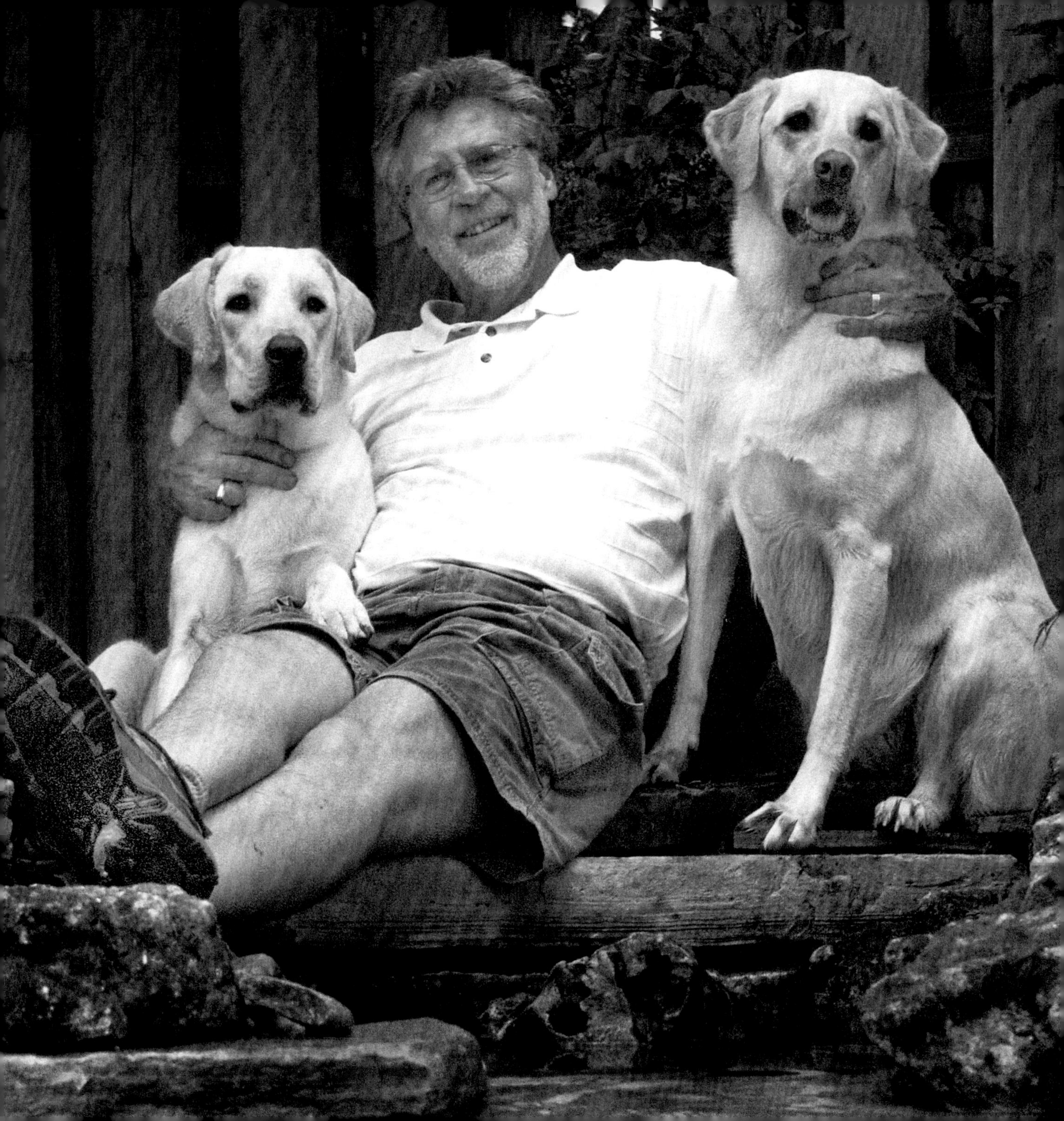

Come on kid,
give me the donut.

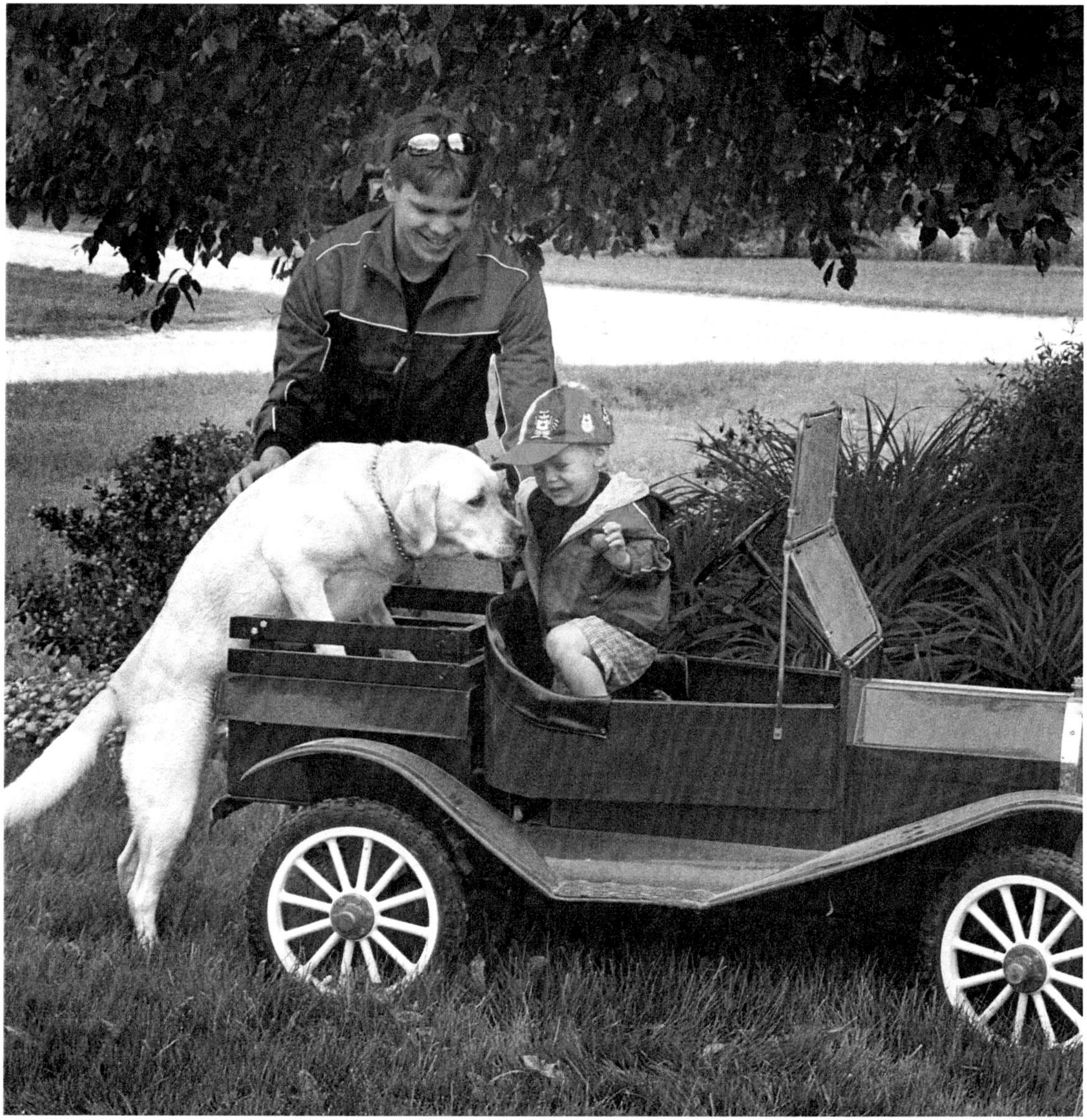

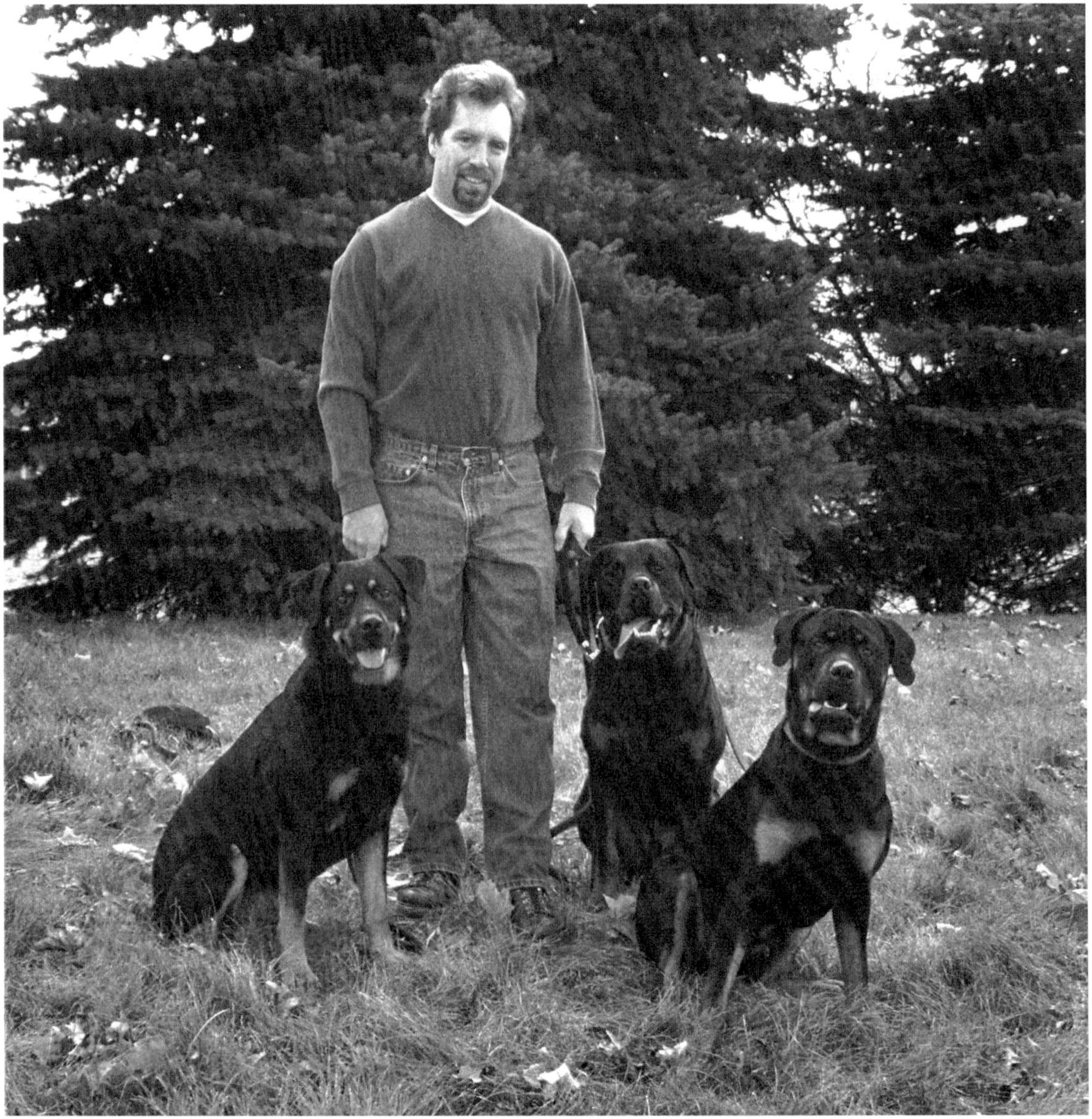

Dogs that no one else wanted
have become loving family members.

I am never allowed to wallow in self-pity
because I have my best friend and a tennis ball.

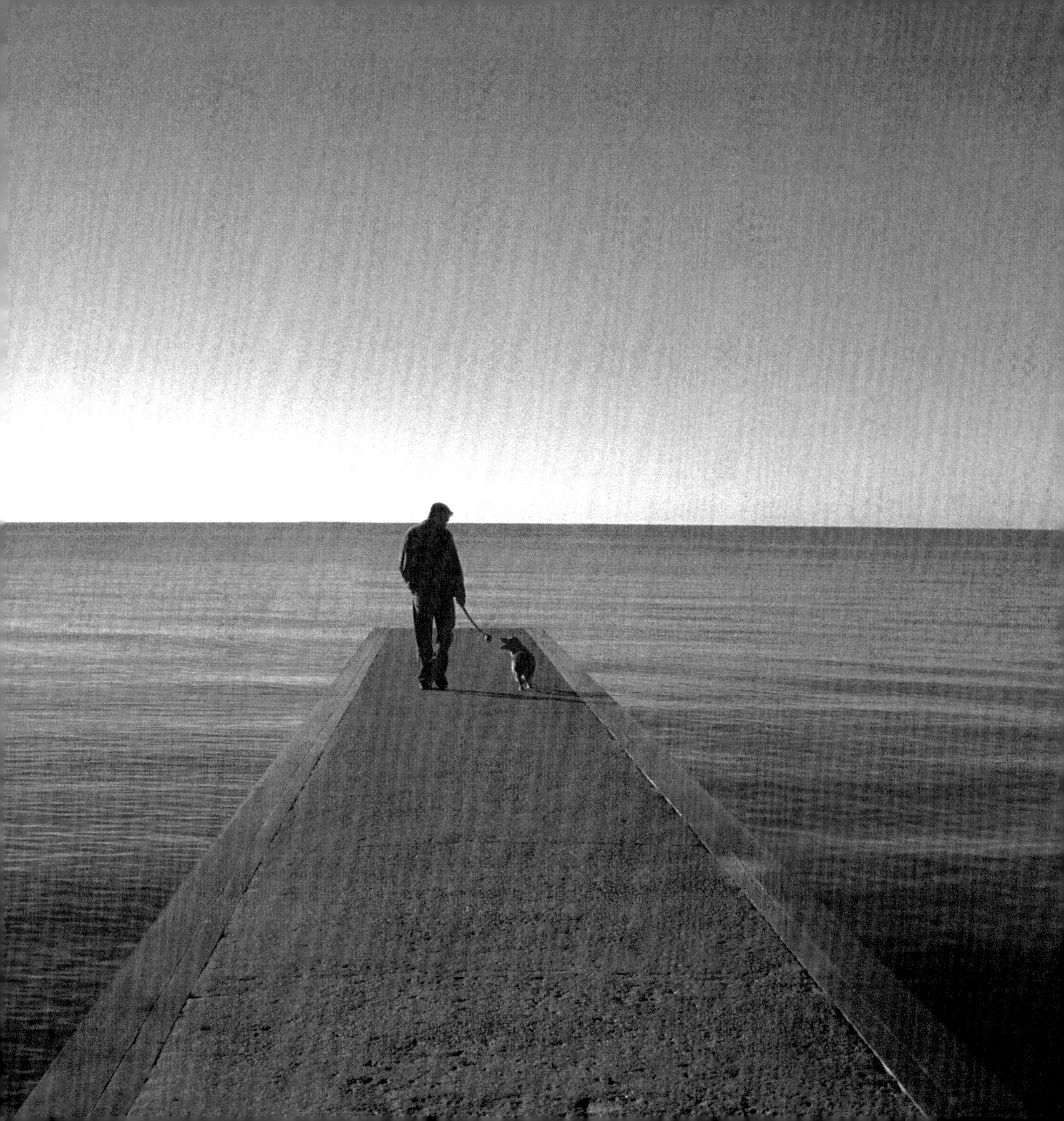

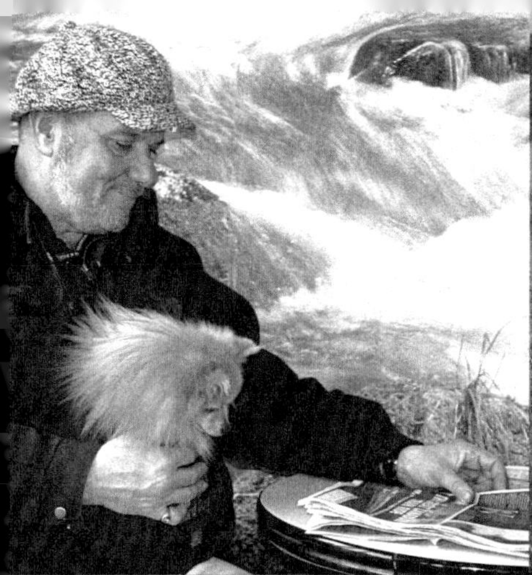
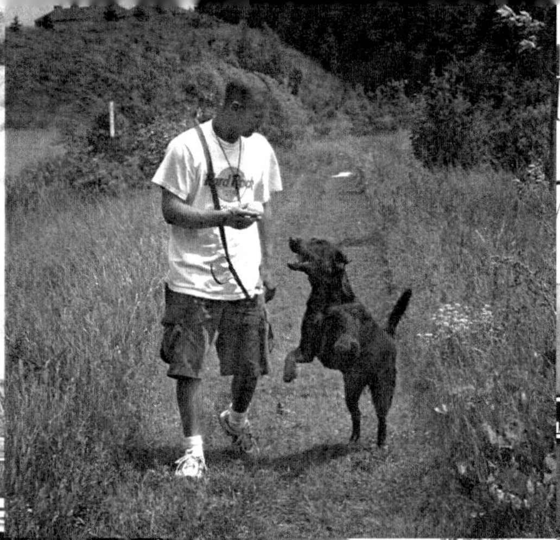
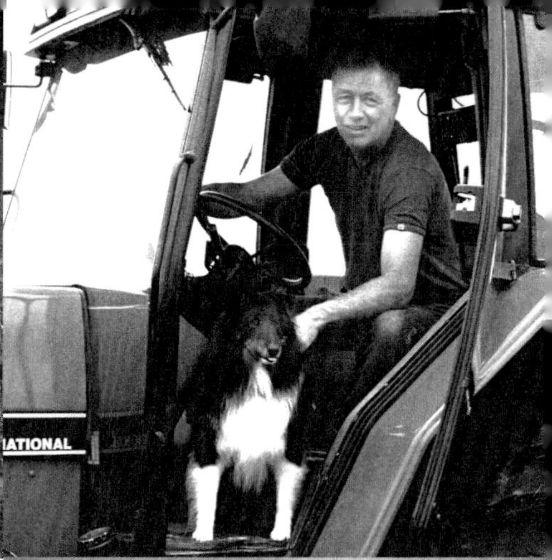
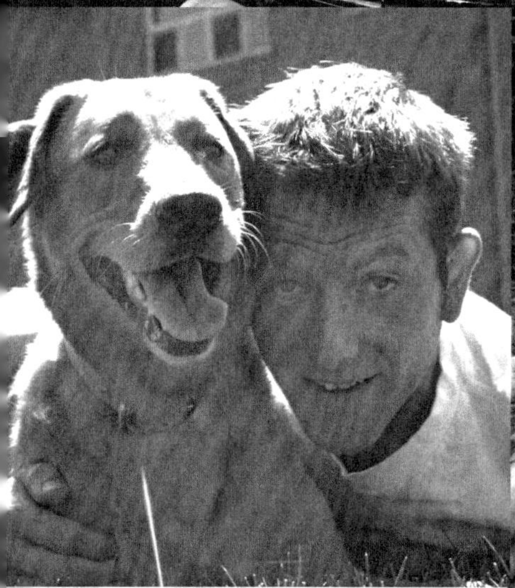
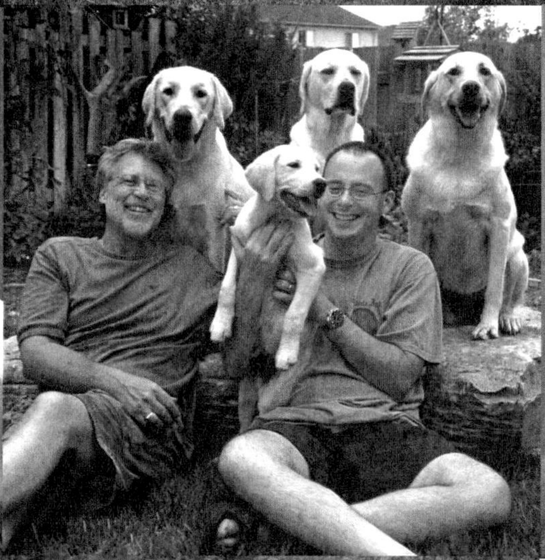
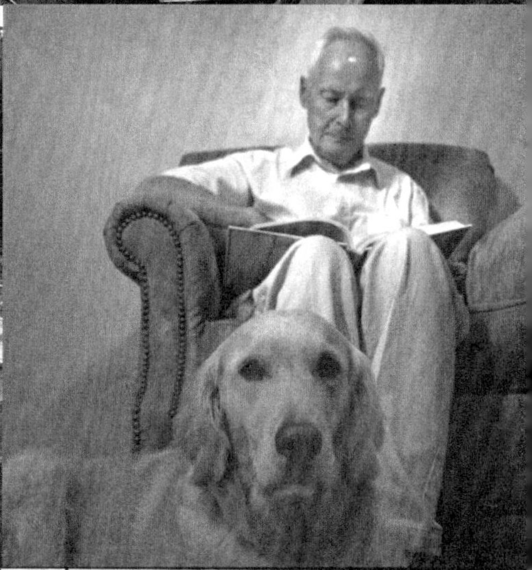
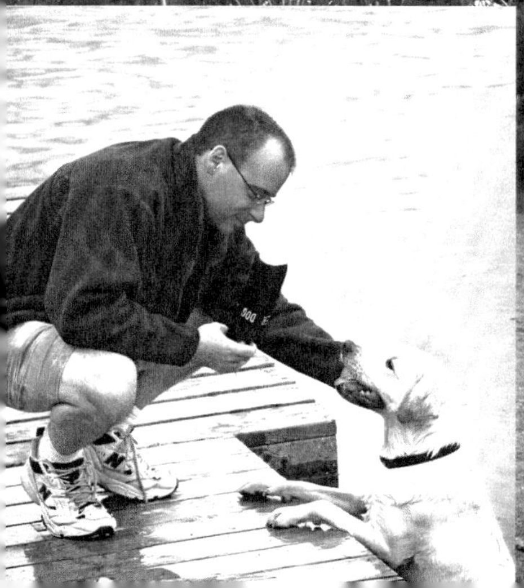
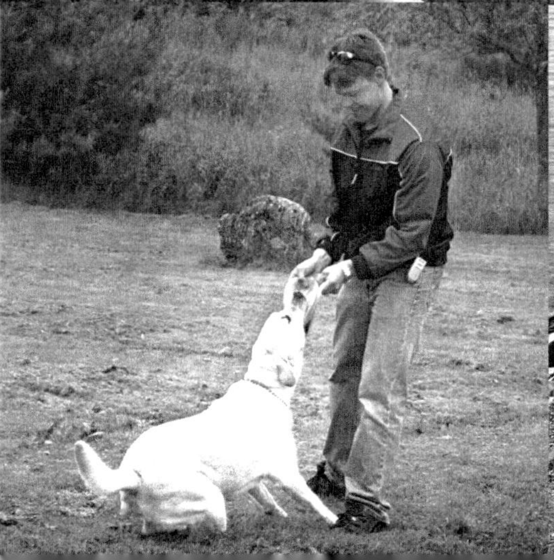
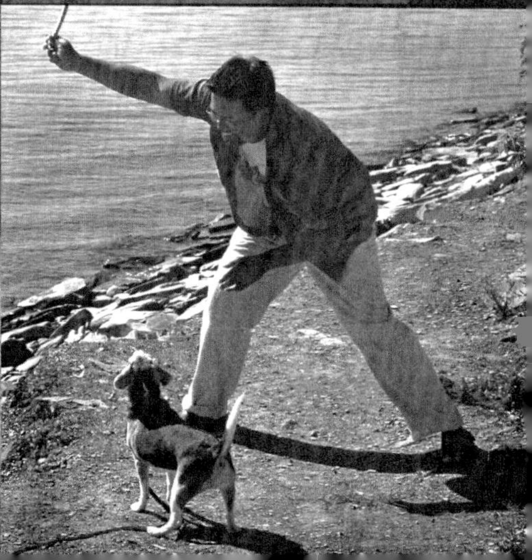

About the Author

A professional journalist and photographer for over 10 years, Sandra Bolan has photographed everything from local tractor pulls and pee-wee hockey games to dignitaries and historical landmarks. But her favourite subject has always been animals. In 2001, she turned her lens on all things canine and has had her photos published on greeting cards and in numerous magazines. She was a 2004 Maxwell Award nominee by the Dog Writers Association of America. Sandra lives in Newmarket, Ontario with her husband, a cat and two yellow Labrador Retrievers.

About the Editors

Jackie Lindsay is a three-time Maxwell award winner for feature editorial from Dog Writers Association of America. She is the founder and former editor of *Dogs, Dogs, Dogs!*, a Toronto-based newspaper for dog lovers. Jackie lives in Toronto with her husband, two cats and two Golden Retrievers.

Brian Balogh has been in the photography industry for about 7 years, and has owned his own store for 3. He has a son and lives in the Newmarket, Ontario area. He has a great passion and dedication for his home life, as well as his business.

Acknowledgements

Tucker J. Axton-Nore and Petie; R.C. Pete Ward and Skye; Mark Seaton with Bear and Bella; Stanley J. Gibson and Scampy; Paul Bartlett and Jessie; David Bolan with Wally and Alvin; Bryan Tenenhouse with Brutus and Brady; Rolando Garcia with Carmela and Concha; Michel Lafleche and Cody; Nicolas Lemire and Oliver; Howard Bluwol with Sam and Lola; Michael Boucher and Paddington; Robert Kennedy and Candle; Russ Pagulayan and Zoë; Greg Gourlie and Bo; Shawn Gourlie and Carter; Chris Gourlie and Riley; John Sheppard with Chloe and Molly; Harry Ballard and Toto; Brian Carre and Fusion; Dave Taylor and Madison; Damian Weston and Mokey; Paul Chahivec with Indiana and Hunter; Dennis Alexander and Tango; Jeff Gayman and Rueger; Craig A. Mouldey and Boonie; Larry Goldin with Sito and Tylo; Tyler Mazereeuw with Rory; Tom Harrison and Hank; Ken Grace and Rory; Andrew Grace and Bentley; Gary Masters and Logan; Brian Wallace with Roxie and Diesel; Eren Howell and Jessie; Arthur Newman with Jenny and Ella; Greg Griffin with Nicky and Sebastian; Paul Porter and Suka; Laszlo Takacs and Tully; Nigel Ward-Paige and Britta; Gerry Lebel and Winston; Peter Trebble and Otis; Corey Bayford and Toby; Keith M. Koski with Buddy and Bambi; Keith Linton and Sally; Scott Kennedy and Scottie; Edward Kotlan with Ozzie and Shakira; Larry Stumpf with Toby and Callie; John Michalenko and Sierra; Stephen Alexander with TJ, Frankie and Boone; Rich Kraemer and Kirby.